W9-BTN-711

Continued success
Marketing your Music!

Maxine Brody

Career MAGIC

A Woman's Guide to Reward & Recognition

Marjorie Brody, MA, CSP, CMC

Career MAGIC
A Woman's Guide to Reward & Recognition

Copyright 2004 Career Skills Press

Printed in Winfield, Kansas
United States of America

Any reproduction of any part of this publication without the written permission of Career Skills Press is prohibited.

Edited by: Rosalie M. Doherty & Miryam S. Roddy
Cover design by: George Foster, Foster & Foster

Career Skills Press
815 Greenwood Avenue, Suite 8
Jenkintown, PA 19046 USA
800-726-7936
215-886-1688
Fax: 215-886-1699
E-mail: brody@BrodyCommunications.com
www.BrodyCommunications.com or www.MarjorieBrody.com

Library of Congress Control Number: 2003112258

ISBN 1-931148-09-0

Contents

Acknowledgments

It's well known that women work well collaboratively. This book could not exist without collaboration.

My special thanks go to Rosalie Doherty, who took my words and ideas and made sense of them, and to Miryam S. Roddy, who was the backbone for this project. Miryam's tenacity and hard work coordinating schedules for interviews, compiling information, editing and writing deserve special praise.

To the other women at Brody Communications Ltd. who read this, made suggestions and provided ideas.

To the focus group of women who convinced me it wasn't research but ideas that were needed.

To the highly successful women interviewed for this book — 35 in all — that were willing to share their ideas and time so that *all* women could benefit from their wisdom.

To my female clients, many of whom shared their career frustrations and encouraged me to write this book.

To my women friends who have always been there to support me.

To my daughters, mother and sister who continue to give me unconditional love.

To all my male clients who value the contributions professional women make every day in the workplace, and who recognize the benefit of keeping the work environment gender neutral.

To my husband, Alan, for reminding me what's really important.

Introduction

Don't Wait for Success to Fall in Your Lap, Grab It!

You're hardworking. Dedicated. Smart. But, you're overlooked when it comes to promotions and ignored despite your contributions. You're not getting the opportunities you need to reach your potential. You watch others move forward, full speed ahead, while you get left behind in their wake.

The fact is, when it comes to their careers, women often are not taken seriously. Many times they are taken for granted. According to the "2002 Catalyst Census of Women Corporate Officers and Top Earners," women occupy only 5.2 percent of the highest earning positions in America's largest companies. Only 7.9 percent of the most prestigious titles — chairman, vice chairman, CEO, president, COO, Senior Executive Vice President and Executive Vice President — are held by women. Yet women account for approximately 48 percent of the U.S. workforce.

That's not to say there haven't been breakthroughs. Research by the New York-based Catalyst shows that women have attained higher-level positions in corporate legal, communications and human resources departments. Women are definitely in the race for corporate advancement. But most of them are stopping short of reaching top management levels.

1

Does this sound like the story of your life? Are you wondering why others manage to step into the spotlight, but you get treated like the invisible woman?

I've been there. I know what it's like to have the skill *and will* to do more professionally, but have something — an unknown, hidden barrier — holding me back.

After years of being a popular and successful college professor and working hard at my job, I felt like I was ready and able to accomplish more. The problem was that no one was giving me the opportunity.

I attended conferences and saw people on stage talking about the same topics I was teaching in my classes. I wondered how these people got asked to speak at conferences, but no one ever asked me. Didn't anybody realize I had the knowledge to do this? Couldn't they see I had great potential as a conference speaker?

I also noticed the many books and magazine articles being published on the very same subjects I taught. I wondered how other people got to write about these subjects. I was just as capable, why not me? I even heard the same stuff I was saying in the classroom being discussed on radio and TV shows.

No doubt about it; I felt like a victim. I thought like a victim:

"How did *they* get to do that?"

"Why not *me*?"

I was determined to find out how people were achieving the kind of professional success and recognition that I wanted and deserved. I started researching and observing. And, in the process, I learned how to take my life story and turn it into a masterpiece.

I learned to be *proactive*, not *reactive*. I stopped waiting to be discovered, and started letting the right people know I was capable and interested in doing more.

Opportunity would not come knocking on my door. I realized the need to find and make my own opportunities. Eventually, when I left teaching to launch my training and executive coaching firm, I applied the things I learned. I have been able to build Brody Communications Ltd. into an extremely successful international company. And, yes, I do speak at conferences now, write books and articles, and am interviewed regularly on radio and TV shows. But, most importantly, I've been able to craft my own career and choose its direction.

Why wait any longer? This very day, *you* can begin making changes in the story of your life, as well! These changes will enable you to move forward confidently and creatively, with more self-respect and fewer apologies, and with purpose and passion.

According to a 2003 in-depth study of more than 80 top women leaders conducted by Roslyn Courtney Consulting of New York, leadership started early in the careers of these extraordinary women — long before they were in positions of power. "They revealed unusual leadership potential and capabilities when they were still in their cubicles because they volunteered to solve difficult problems. These women looked for and saw the possibilities to contribute; they helped to develop new and creative solutions and shared ideas to advance the business," Courtney explained. "They felt strongly committed to making a difference." Many of the leaders in her study are CEOs, or run major businesses/departments, or run their own successful companies.

I'm not saying that it's necessary for you to aim for the top leadership position at your company or within your industry. Just go for what you desire — if it's a larger role in the marketing department, that's fine. Or, perhaps you want the title "Vice President" — terrific. *Any goal is obtainable once you set your sights on it.*

You may wonder how to make changes in your current job situation. There is a way to make this a "magical" process. I use the acronym MAGIC to define the steps that will lead you toward the mastery of an effective personal marketing plan. And a marketing plan is exactly what you need to achieve practically any professional goal!

You can be great at what you do, but if others are unaware of your abilities and contributions, your true value may never be discovered. The people blasting past you on the road to success are probably not working harder or more intelligently at their jobs. But, you can be sure they are doing fantastic personal marketing. They are spending the time and effort to do things that get recognition and respect.

I have many clients who are working hard but not getting ahead, and they often ask me for help with their professional development. After I listened to one client describe her outstanding work contributions, my first question was, "Does your manager know you are doing that?" I heard another woman describe her frustration at not reaching her potential and asked, "Is your manager aware of your professional goals?" It's astounding how often the response to these questions is, "No." That's when I know that these women's real problem is the lack of a personal marketing plan.

Remember, your manager isn't a mind reader. The people holding the keys to the doors you want opened in your career are not mind readers. You *must* let them know what you do and what you want.

It's not unusual for a corporation to spend millions of dollars every year on a marketing plan that creates and advertises a carefully selected image, an image that makes the outside world notice and desire what that business has to offer. The companies you work for have marketing and sales budgets because their products and services won't be in demand, regardless of how good they are, if people don't know about them and what makes them unique.

The same is true for you. You are a product — you are hard work, creativity and intelligence personified! And ***it's high time you started marketing yourself and your wonderful qualities and boundless potential as one awesome, impressive product, just like you would any other product you believed in.***

Like any effective marketing effort, your personal campaign will focus on understanding, creating, communicating and delivering value to your "customer" — the people who can give you access to your career goals. And like any effective marketing plan, you already have a "differential advantage," a unique feature that sets the product — you — apart from the competition: it's your own, unique magic!

But you have to know how to market your magic. This book will show you how, using the five important components of my **MAGIC** formula. Your **MAGIC** is all about your:

M — Manner. This is the impression you make and how you communicate with others. Also, add an "s" to manner. Your manners matter. I will discuss how common courtesies, or lack of them, can affect your career.

A — Advocates. Advocates are people who can hire you, recommend you, or introduce you to others. You must find ways to meet and develop relationships with people who will be your advocates.

G — Growth. In order to develop professionally, you must continually investigate ways to grow. This includes determining what skills and knowledge you should acquire, and what risks you should consider taking to achieve your goals.

I — Involvement. Get involved in organizations and seek leadership positions that will give you the most visibility.

C — Commentary. Seek opportunities to give commentary through writing and speaking engagements. This will help you get established as an expert in your field.

Developing in each of these areas is essential to developing your career. The principles apply to virtually anyone, regardless of position or industry. However, undertaking a conscious, strategic personal marketing effort is something that seems to cause many women to struggle.

For years, I've been speaking about personal marketing and sharing my **MAGIC** formula with both men and women, and it's the women, by far, who need more perspective and coaching with it. A woman is more likely to think, "I'm doing a good job, shouldn't that be enough?" The answer is a resounding, "No!" Men are much better at tooting their own horns, much more aware of the need to market themselves, and much more strategic when doing so.

Therefore, although the principles of my **MAGIC** formula apply to both genders, I've written this book for women. In it, I will define the barriers to personal marketing and self-promotion that women face, or that they create for themselves. I will show you how to develop the **MAGIC** within you and make your career goals become a reality.

I also share the input and experiences of many wonderful, "magical," and amazingly successful women who tell their stories to encourage and help other women. Like me, they want to see more women achieve fulfillment in their careers. They are women of outstanding professional status from more than 30 different industries. They range in age from 30 to 65. Some are married, some are not. Some have children, others do not. Some were strategic in planning their careers, others relied more on their instincts or intuition.

These women helped me test my **MAGIC** formula. Through our interviews, I found that many of them intuitively or strategically use the **MAGIC** principles. I will share their insights and examples of strategies that worked for them in building their careers.

I still rely on the five marketing and promotional components of the **MAGIC** formula as I continue on my career path. I'm constantly fine-tuning and making personal improvements. Along the way, I'm also enjoying the accolades and triumphs I have earned.

My objective for this book is that it will help you achieve your professional triumphs. I want to reinforce what you are doing right, and encourage you to do more of it. But I also want to offer insights that can help you change self-limiting attitudes and behaviors.

It's never too late, or too early, to launch your **MAGIC** plan. Keep reading and start making your own magic!

Chapter 1
If It's Meant to Be, It's Up to Me

When you market your magic, you're showing the world you are the real deal and you've got a lot to offer. This chapter will help you get tuned into the authentic, unique individual you were meant to be, then show you how to find out if that's what others actually see.

Let's start by taking a good look at what you really want to achieve!

Where Am I Going?

How far have you come in the race for career success and recognition? If you're like many women, not as far as you want, or feel you deserve.

Over half of the women executives I surveyed for this book were dissatisfied with their opportunities to develop professionally. Many felt they were not being recognized for their contributions.

So, if you're feeling left out or left behind, you're not alone. The good news is, you're not out of the running and the race isn't over yet!

But wait just a moment. What exactly are you going after? Hopefully, it's something you enjoy pursuing, something that highlights your special talents and offers personal fulfillment, because that's what success is all about … right?

Only you can decide what success means to you. You may be a woman whose goal is to break through barriers to career advancement, all the way through the proverbial glass ceiling. Or, you may want the choices and flexibility of being your own boss. You may want to start a new business that highlights your unique talents and enables you to focus more on family and other aspects of your life.

True success requires getting on the right track, not necessarily the fast track. Be willing to slow down and change lanes in order to achieve your real goals.

For example, if your dream is to open your own restaurant, you're not getting any closer to achieving that dream if all your time and effort is spent positioning yourself as your company's next CEO. Imagine what you could do if you put all that energy into getting what you really want out of life! Perhaps raising a family is your priority. Then why take on a career that requires a lot of travel? Is that aspect of the job going to change? If not, start your own business, be your own boss, get the career that enables you to do what really matters to you. Do you want the freedom to express yourself with flamboyant clothing and hairstyles? You can't do that in a button-down, corporate environment. Decide what's more important — the job or the style. Then make the change that's right for you.

You want the challenge and satisfaction of being a corporate boss? Then take the steps you need to stand out and get noticed. You can be the one who takes the company and turns it around, who uses her experience and knowledge to get ahead in a male-dominated business world.

The point is, *be preemptive in your thinking*. Don't wait to get noticed, and certainly don't start, or remain in, a career that causes you to sacrifice or delay getting what you really want from life. True success is more than a paycheck or a job title or a corner office. It starts with knowing *you* have value; you have a purpose in life that goes far beyond any glass ceiling you may encounter. Don't waste time getting ahead, only to find you didn't end up where you wanted to be.

What's Stopping Me?

Brody Communications Ltd. surveyed 308 professionals in the fall of 2002 about their self-marketing efforts, or lack thereof. *Of 171 women* who responded, *more than half — 56% percent — admitted they were confused about self-marketing* and wished they could get more details about what the concept means and guidance on how to do it. Interestingly, *only 40% of males surveyed said they were confused about self-marketing and needed help.*

So why do women refuse to do effective self-marketing or have a difficult time doing it? The top five reasons why those surveyed don't use self-marketing strategies were: "not sure what to do (19.3%)," followed by "lack of confidence (6.4%)," "happy in current role (5.9%)" "not necessary (5.3%)" and "no reason, just don't (4.7%)."

My philosophy is that women are experts at convincing themselves that they can't achieve the level of

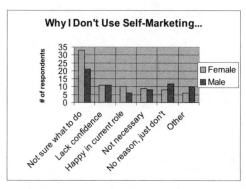

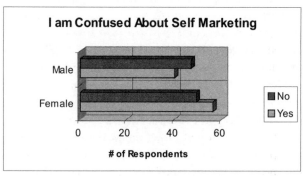

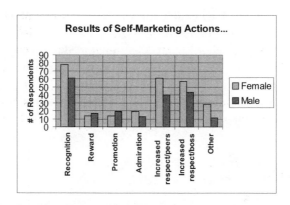

Statistics from a 2003 Brody Communications Ltd. survey of 308 professionals (171 women, 137 men) in a variety of industries, including financial, government, pharmaceuticals, beverage, computer, defense and manufacturing.

personal fulfillment they want. It happens to all of us at one time or another. There's an inner voice that deceives us into thinking we can't achieve more because we are flawed, limited, unable, or destined to fail. The voice says we aren't good enough, or experienced enough. It tells us to be quiet, don't interrupt, don't make waves. It causes us to fear, to be paralyzed, to become unable to demand respect or take a stand.

That voice isn't coming from a good place.

It robs you of your potential. It is incorrect thinking, and it prevents you from becoming the unique person you were meant to be. If you allow negative thoughts to hold you back, you have built your own barrier to true success. Make up your mind to knock that barrier down. Get those ideas out of your head and start thinking about what you can do, instead.

Here are five examples of wrong ideas that many women have bought into which prevent them from achieving their full career potential.

Wrong Idea #1:
It's better to be safe than sorry.

Well, yes, if it's a life or death issue. But when it comes to getting more from your career, what's the worst that can happen if you take a risk? Focus on succeeding, not failing. Be determined to learn and grow from every experience, regardless of the outcome. Then jump in and hit the ground running.

Follow the example of Bill Gates, who not only guided Microsoft to skyrocketing success over the past two decades, but also changed the world with easy-to-use, accessible computer technology. Gates' philosophy was to develop the product quickly and get it out on the market: Start selling it, get people to use it and rely on it, then you'll learn what needs to be fixed for the next version.

Use this attitude in your own career strategy. Start marketing yourself now. Refuse to remain stagnant. By taking action, asking for what you want and going after it, you will become open and available in your career and life. You will learn what works, and what doesn't, in your own self-marketing strategy and thus be able to make the necessary adjustments.

Brody Communications Ltd.'s survey shows that there *are* measurable results when women use self-marketing strategies. The top three results chosen were: 78% received recognition of some kind, 61% also saw increased respect among peers and colleagues, and 57% said their bosses and superiors held them in higher esteem.

So don't wait. Start thinking about how you can improve your self-marketing tactics. Your efforts will be rewarded. The willingness to take risks is a characteristic shared by many successful women.

Jeanie Duck, Senior Vice President of The Boston Consulting Group, says she is "a huge risk-taker. I'm willing to jump in even when I'm not sure I'm ready." Duck is author of the book *Change Monster: The Human Forces that Fuel or Foil Corporate Transformation and Change.*

"Be willing to take risks in your roles," said Peggi Einhorn, Senior Vice President, JPMorganChase. Being flexible and willing to change jobs has helped her career and led to promotions. She says that if your role isn't moving you in the right direction, make a change, even if it means taking a lateral move. "You don't always have to be promoted when making a move," Einhorn said.

"Seize opportunities when they come your way," said Ada C. Nielsen, Manager, Commercial Development, Nitriles Licensing, for BP Chemicals.

Wrong Idea #2:
I have to be perfect.

Many women feel they have to be perfect. The problem is, you are not, and *never* will be, perfect. No one is. You will make mistakes, and you should be accountable and try to fix what you can. But to achieve your potential, you have to be willing to accept your own mistakes. It's OK to mess up once in a while. If you deal with any business *faux pas* properly, others will get over it and you should, too.

It's OK to aspire to perfection. Just don't let perfectionism stop you or slow you down. If you do, you will never fulfill your true potential.

Wrong Idea #3:
I'm not good enough ... I don't have enough experience ... I haven't had the job long enough ...

Enough nonsense!

Stop procrastinating. If you are stuck in a mindset of "getting ready to get ready," or waiting for the time to be "right," you are wasting time and limiting your potential.

You cannot achieve a goal without doing something about it today. So, get started!

It's time to stretch. Push past self-imposed limitations. If you need to further your education, start taking classes. If you need to start putting your education to work, then get a job that relates to what you've learned. If you have a vision for your career, create opportunities that will make it a reality. Take the next step and take on the challenges that will help you achieve your goals.

Sheryl Craun, Vice President of Client Services at ADP Retirement Services, said that by challenging herself, she achieved career success. "I stretched. I pulled up strengths I didn't know I had, and found I went further than I thought I could," she said. In doing this, Craun also learned what her limitations were and how to manage and improve them. After all, if you don't try, how do you know what you need to improve?

Craun has built her career by believing in herself and inspiring others to believe in her, too. In college, she created her own internship, cold-called potential employers about the position and landed a job at Sun Company. A few years later, while just a training manager at Vanguard, Craun convinced her employer that she was the right candidate to open a new office in another city. "I said, 'Give me a chance.' They did." The lesson learned from her career path? "Ask for what you want, and prove yourself," Craun said.

I urge you not to wait until you are finished reading this book to use my advice and the words of wisdom from the many successful women I interviewed. Read a few pages at a time, or a chapter at a time, while putting the ideas into practice. Evaluate what you are doing and how you are doing it, and *take action*.

Try something new each day and enjoy the remarkable changes in your attitude and your career.

Wrong Idea #4:
Good things happen to those who wait.

I say good things happen to those *who go after them!* Those who wait get the leftovers.

Women often enter the workforce with an internal value system that emphasizes qualities such as service and generosity. Unfortunately, many women interpret these qualities to mean being passive and overly patient, and therefore develop a self-limiting type of work ethic. These women think that if they work hard and are nice to others, they will get the recognition they deserve. When it comes to your career development, that attitude doesn't work, especially not in our male-dominated environment that emphasizes a different set of values — obtaining power and control.

This attitude of working hard and waiting patiently for a reward causes women to become invisible in the workplace. It prevents women from standing up for themselves. It makes them reluctant to demand respect, to assert their ideas. It's the "Cellophane Man" song from the musical *Chicago*, played out in real life.

This attitude will not get people to be advocates for you, or to respect what you say when you finally decide it's time to take a stand. It will make you a doormat.

"You can never cruise; you have no choice," said Karen Daroff, President of Daroff Design Inc. in Philadelphia. "You can never stop marketing or selling."

Look at the people in your company, or anyone for that matter, who you consider successful. Are they working harder than you? Are they smarter or more talented than you? Nicer than you? Probably not! The difference is that they are doing a better job of self-marketing. They are taking the time and making the effort to do things beyond work, things that get them noticed.

"You need to let people know what you have accomplished," said Irene Horstmann Hannan, Senior Vice President & Director, Women's Business Services, at Wachovia. "Don't wait for your manager to recognize what you've done. He will not see your passiveness as an attribute."

Success isn't going to come to you. You have to go after it. Don't be a victim. Take the controls, be accountable. Get noticed. Spend time getting to know people. Tell others what you are working toward. Contribute at meetings. Don't be afraid to interrupt or take a stand.

Continue to find meaning in your work by providing excellent service. Continue to be a caring and generous person who respects others — but show self-respect and make sure you get the recognition that you deserve, too.

Wrong Idea #5:
I have to do it all, all by myself.

Women truly get stuck with the mindset of trying to do it all, all by themselves. An otherwise career-minded woman will take on a task and plug away at every detail alone. She may do this for different reasons, none of them right: She doesn't want to bother others; she feels it's her duty; she thinks no one else will do the job right.

It's important to be independent, to be a self-starter. But, it's also important to know when to include others in your efforts. Ask for help when you need it. The job or project may get done better, or faster, with the input of others. You will feel less stressed, and you'll have the time and energy to accomplish even more. It's also a good career move to include colleagues in your efforts. In many work environments, employees are expected to be team players. Working together enables you to build valuable relationships and alliances.

Fight the tendency to try to do it all on your own. It's not a good way to get things done and it limits your potential.

Does My Hard Work Really Matter?

So far, I've discussed setting goals for a career that truly offers you personal fulfillment, and letting go of the wrong ideas that are holding you back. These things are essential in order for you to start marketing your "magic." Equally important is your track record as a contributor. Results matter tremendously in establishing a solid foundation for your self-marketing efforts.

If you don't have a reputation for getting the job done, for being reliable and meeting deadlines, it won't make a bit of difference that you have a positive attitude and know what you want. Like any product, you must have value as an employee if you are going to market yourself to your employer successfully.

Roll up your sleeves and do what it takes to get the job done. It's even better for your track record if the job or project is a significant, highly visible one. Volunteer for the tough assignments.

"Take on difficult tasks and be successful at them," said Horstmann Hannan. "Don't always do what's comfortable. Do what will get you attention. Women have to work harder to achieve the same recognition as men." She advises women to be strategic in their efforts to advance their careers. "Women might put out information about themselves, but they don't connect the dots. I connect the dots. Everything I do is a means to an end."

Work hard, but work smart. Don't let mundane tasks divert your efforts from important work that will enhance your track record and give you visibility. When you see an opportunity to shine, grab it. When a crisis occurs, let the other stuff wait. A crisis can be a career opportunity in disguise. Handle the challenge with confidence and competence.

Lynn A. Tetrault, Vice President Human Resources at AstraZeneca, said the key to her career success was "to be at the helm and take major responsibilities when a crisis occurred. In one instance, I handled the media spotlight and took a strong role to guide the work." Her advice to women: "Don't shrink away from responsibility.

Don't be afraid to take on challenges. This is what gives you visibility."

How Do Others Describe Me?

You're a valuable employee who works hard. You have a clear vision of your goals. To reach them, you're going to get rid of self-limiting ideas that create internal barriers.

Now, take a realistic look at your image. How do others perceive you? Don't assume! Get honest feedback in order to present an image that reflects your strengths and maximizes your potential.

As part of my executive coaching, I do "360-degree" interviews. I ask the individual being coached to tell me how others would describe him or her, then I talk to supervisors, colleagues, peers, customers and subordinates, and ask them key questions in order to get honest, thoughtful feedback pertaining to that individual.

You can do a similar self-evaluation. Use the following worksheet. In the first column, make a list of the words you would like people to use in describing you. Next, ask people who know you to list words that they feel best describe you. Ask them to be completely candid in identifying your strengths as well as your limitations. Write their words in the second column.

Assessment Exercise

What Do I Want People to Say About Me?	What Do They Actually Say?

Now, compare the two columns. Do any of their words match yours? Where are the gaps, the areas of their descriptions that don't match yours? These gaps enable you to identify aspects of your image that may be preventing you from reaching your potential. Once you have this information, you can take the steps necessary for improvement.

Here is an example of a similar evaluation I conducted for Barbara, a pharmaceutical executive who wanted to improve her image:

What Do I Want People to Say About Me?	What Do They Actually Say?
Friendly	Aloof
Good communicator	Doesn't take the time to interact properly
Smart	Smart
Caring	Conscientious
Conscientious	

The good news for Barbara is that people *do* consider her to be smart and conscientious, two of the words she hoped they would use to describe her. The gaps in this evaluation are between Barbara's desire to be friendly, caring and a good communicator, and the reality that people consider her to be aloof and abrupt. Now that Barbara knows about the gaps, however, she can take steps to bridge them. She is making changes in her attitude that focus on improving her interpersonal skills. This will help Barbara with her self-marketing efforts and career advancement goals.

Information is power! Get the honest feedback you need to begin your own self-marketing efforts. Focus on cultivating the personality traits of successful women. The female executives I interviewed used the following words to describe themselves:

- optimistic
- resourceful
- confident
- courageous
- dynamic
- enthusiastic
- interesting
- outgoing
- caring
- sincere

These attributes are the fuel for a positive professional image. They determine how you present yourself, treat others, and tackle your job responsibilities.

For example, if you are sincere, you will follow through with commitments and others will trust you. If you are caring, you will make the employees on your team feel like they belong. If you are optimistic and resourceful, others will see you as the person to count on for the top assignments. If you respect yourself and others, you will dress and act professionally.

Your exterior package is a reflection of your character and personality. If you are a positive, confident, "can-do" individual, you will be able to light up a room with your energy and enthusiasm. If you lack confidence and have a poor self-concept, you're likely to make others doubt your abilities as well. What you are on the inside shows on the outside. Start thinking of yourself in positive ways and others will, too!

Self-marketing strategies shouldn't be considered the magical panacea to career success. Judith E. Tschirgi, Chief Information Officer & Senior Vice President, for SEI Investments, said, "Self promotion is a byproduct of your business agenda — not an end in itself."

Remember, the real you is behind the marketing magic. Believe it, and *be* it!

Chapter 2 ~ M
Your Magic Starts with Your Manner

Your manner is the first and most important part of my **MAGIC** formula. Your manner is how you present yourself to other people.

It includes that oh-so-important first impression and extends to maintaining the right impression in your daily interactions with coworkers and managers. But it goes so much deeper! It's how people think about you. It's your most important self-marketing tool.

Let's start with your exterior package: the way you look, act and speak. These aspects are the easiest to improve and control.

I will also address your manners — your professional behavior. Changes in this area of your life can be hard work.

See the sidebar on the next page for coaching opportunities. Can you identify with any of these?

Avoid These Manner Mistakes

Consider the lists below carefully. Do any of the behaviors
pertain to you? These things will give you a bad reputation,
limit your self-promotional efforts, and keep you from career
advancement.

A study by a British recruiting firm of 1,000 office workers
would likely yield the same results if done in America.
Respondents were asked what irritated them about coworkers.

- Six out of 10 said their colleagues never said "Good Morning."

- Eight out 10 said coworkers leave cell phones on at meetings.

- Three out of four complained that others failed to add paper to
  the tray or fix jams with the photocopier, printer or fax.

According to an article in the January 2001 issue of T+D
magazine, MJN Consulting conducted a survey of 500 office
professionals and asked them to rank the top 10 common office
discourtesies according to their aggravation level. They are:

1) not returning phone calls, voice mail, e-mail or pages in
   a timely manner

2) using the last piece of paper in the printer or copier and
   not refilling it

3) showing up late to meetings or answering cell phones

4) making a mess of the microwave and not cleaning it up

5) setting the copy machine for special features and not
   changing it back

6) cruising the office visiting people instead of working

7) clogging e-mail with long messages, jokes and
   downloads

8) borrowing co-workers' supplies and not returning them

9) taking the last cup of coffee and not making more

10) playing the radio or CDs too loudly or constantly

With a poor manner, you don't have a fighting chance. A poor manner *closes* doors. In this part of the MAGIC formula, I will show you how to make the changes that will open them.

There are three components of your manner to consider: visual, verbal and vocal. Then, there are the behavioral aspects, which are often not as immediately apparent.

Your Visual Manner

How do you look?

Think of the marketing materials used by the companies you have worked for and the companies you'd like to work for. Successful companies market themselves carefully through Web sites, brochures, product packages and advertising. They invest a great deal of time and money developing the right image. You should cultivate your own image just as carefully.

Far too many women get stuck on the corporate ladder, or never even start the climb, because of their professional manner. Unfortunately, many women don't even know that shortcomings in their manner may be what's holding them back.

Your manner includes your visual impact on people — your appearance and body language. When you maintain an impeccable visual appearance, your self-worth is shining through. You are showing people that you've got it together personally and professionally.

In addition, you're setting a good example for the other employees on your team. For these reasons, you should always be motivated to look your best.

Margery Geers, Vice President, Human Resources, Healthcare Management Services, at Aramark Corp., knows the importance of looking great, and the consequences when that doesn't happen. "My manner has helped me. I always ensure that I am well groomed and dressed." She learned the importance of visual appearance after an incident early in her career when Geers wore a dress that was a bit too form-fitting when giving a presentation. She was so uncomfortable that she couldn't come out from behind the lectern, and gave a poor presentation due to lack of confidence.

In my experience as an executive coach, it's definitely the little things that stop people from being marketable. Often, an employee is clueless that her visual appearance is offensive to others. She may not understand the impact and consequences of her dress, body language and grooming. Fortunately, improvements in these areas are among the easiest ways to enhance your professional manner. But to address the problem, you first need to be aware of it. Certainly, you should be aware of your dress and grooming habits with the goal to look like a polished professional. You should also be open to feedback. Ask a trusted friend or coworker if you look the part.

Several years ago, I got a call from a managing director at a large accounting firm. He told me there was a woman at the firm who was hard working, talented and smart. She deserved to be made a partner. "But she doesn't look the part," he said.

The managing director went on to describe her to me. I asked him if he had taken the first and most important step in addressing the problem: "Have you ever given her this feedback?" He stuttered and stammered. Obviously, the answer was "no." I suggested he give her the appropriate feedback and discuss how her appearance was limiting her career. Then, if she was willing to meet with me for additional feedback and advice, I would be happy to do so. If she was resistant to change, there was no reason to invest her time and the company's money in a professional consultation.

A month later, the managing director called again and told me the employee wanted to meet with me. When I arrived, I was shocked by the woman's extremely unkempt appearance. I couldn't believe how badly groomed and dressed she was. She was clad entirely in mismatched shades of navy blue, right down to her shoes. The heels on these shoes were entirely worn down, her stockings had a run, her suit was about three sizes too small (the seams were badly stretching), and her blouse was missing a button. Her blond hair was disheveled and over-teased. There was dandruff on her shoulders. Her fingernails were bitten almost down to the quick.

Sounds exaggerated, right? It's not!

We sat across a conference table from each other. I asked, "Do you know why I am here?" She said she didn't. Apparently, the managing director had been too uncomfortable to give this woman the feedback on her appearance to prepare her for our meeting, as I had suggested. I pulled out a set of the "tools" I use for executive presence coaching: two bars of soap, one well-wrapped and the other in a torn and tattered wrapper.

"Which of these bars of soap would you buy if you found them in a market?" I asked. Without hesitation, she selected the one that was well-packaged. I told her I was there to discuss her own "packaging" because it was holding her back.

Her reaction? She was furious. Why? No one had ever given her the feedback she could have used to make improvements. She was encouraged to work hard, to demonstrate her technical and business acumen, but was never given a clue that her appearance was flawed.

After reading this story, you might be wondering three things:

1. How could the employee be unaware that her messy and badly groomed appearance was offensive to others and damaging her career? If you weren't brought up in a household where good grooming and dress were important, you might not understand how much your appearance matters in the business world.

2. Why wasn't she told that her appearance was holding her back? Because it's uncomfortable and embarrassing to give a person negative feedback about his or her appearance, especially when it's

someone of the opposite gender. The male managers who contact me say they find it impossible to tell female employees to correct poor grooming and dress habits. There is also a concern that companies may be sued. The problem is, the employee should be given the opportunity to make improvements. In this instance, the woman at the accounting firm probably does not want to appear poorly groomed or dressed — she simply doesn't realize what she's doing wrong, or that it has damaging consequences to her career.

3. How important is appearance? It's like the cover on this book. An interesting, attractive cover gets you to buy the book, open it and start reading. Similarly, professional appearance shows people you've got a lot to offer, that you are marketable and know how to market something. Your appearance creates an impression of whether or not you are capable of handling a job. For example, a woman I know inherited a sum of money and was interviewing several highly regarded financial planners. On paper, all looked good. Unfortunately, the one my friend thought she would use came late to their meeting, looking totally disheveled, with papers falling out of her briefcase. My friend thought, "How can I hire her? If she can't pay attention to the details of her appearance, how can she pay attention to the details of my account?" Your appearance can be a deal maker, or a deal breaker.

Avoid being passed over for the job you want because of something as easily improved as your appearance. Check yourself out in a full-length mirror and do a frank self-appraisal. Know that people may not approach you about how you look because it is an awkward and difficult subject. So, be proactive! Get honest feedback from people close to you. Observe men and women in your organization, especially those who get recognized and rewarded. They probably "look the part." *You* should, too.

How should you look?

How do you want people to see you? As creative, or serious? Stylish, or conservative?

Today, more than ever before, women in the workplace have the freedom to express their personalities through their clothing choices.

Gone are the days when women were expected to wear masculine business suits. Now, there are more fashion options for female executives. Designers produce attractive, business-appropriate clothing that gives you the opportunity to express yourself and create your own personal style. Your style should tell the corporate world who you are. It should also make the point that you are someone to be taken seriously!

Express yourself, but keep in mind the standards of your work environment and your role. That's where things might get confusing. A suit used to be a safe choice.

In many cases, it still is. Today's suits for women come in a wide variety of styles, colors and prints, and are often appropriate for mixing and matching, so you can experiment and create the look you want. But the business casual look can be harder to put together properly. If this is the standard at your job, be sure to wear only better, dressier, casual clothing.

With so many choices, take care that you do not become a victim of fashion — your career could be the real victim. Although I seem to be swimming upstream against the fashion "current," I am convinced that it is in your best interest to limit the amount of skin you show.

"I wouldn't be caught dead in cropped and sleeveless clothes, even though it seems acceptable," said Sheryl Craun, Vice President of Client Services of ADP Retirement Services.

There is no reason to look like men, but being overly frilly, sexy or "girly" just doesn't cut it. Wearing sleeveless and low-cut items — not to mention skirts that hike up when you are seated — is inappropriate for business. Open-toed sandals are also inappropriate for business. Stockings — even in the summer — are essential.

"I've seen women dress too provocatively and lose business as a result," said Kim Woodworth, Divisional Vice President, Comcast Advertising Sales, Comcast Corp.

It is better to dress on the conservative side. Are there exceptions? Yes, depending on geographical and cultural considerations, corporate standards, and your position. You also will have more or less flexibility in choosing clothing, depending on the industry you are in. Can you be more flamboyant? Yes, if your work ethic and contributions are excellent.

Look around at the women with seniority in your organization. Are there some good role models for dressing appropriately? If advancement is part of your vision, dress to fit higher positions. What you choose to wear is more important than you might want to think. Poor clothing choices often reflect poor judgment. Wearing something that is inappropriate for the occasion can be career limiting. Virtually every successful woman I interviewed for this book emphasized the importance of dress and grooming in projecting a professional image.

Wearing clothes that are dirty, torn, wrinkled or smelly is inexcusable — so is wearing clothes that are either too big or too tight. Go through your wardrobe, making sure that your clothing fits your current body size. If your size has changed, a trip to the tailor for alterations can be a less expensive option than buying new clothes.

Always buy the best quality of clothing you can afford — just buy less. The better the quality, the longer it will last and the better it will look.

Michelle A. Rosen, Senior Director Strategy, Business Development, for McDonald's Corporation, said, "Corporate America is a man's world. Putting your best foot forward includes fashion. Dressing for success is just as important as what you have to say. It's all one package, so spend money on quality, classic fashion items to be a timeless expression of who you are and what you say."

Don't neglect the details! Your shoes should be polished and in good shape. A regional manager of a large pharmaceutical firm told me that shoes are the first thing he looks at when interviewing sales reps. If the heels are worn down or the shoes aren't polished, it's a big mark against the candidate.

He isn't alone. One executive I interviewed said she *always* checks out details like shoes and watches when forming an impression of people. This woman feels people make a good impression when they wear good, tasteful clothes and accessories.

Don't cause clients or customers to think you are extravagant or even controversial. Suzanne F. Fairlie, CPC, President of Pro Search, Inc., is an entrepreneur with her own headhunting firm. She recalls the time she wore a mink coat to a meeting with a client. "The client said, 'I don't like my fees going on your back.'" Fairlie learned her lesson. It's better to play it safe and dress conservatively, rather than extravagantly.

Save the mink for evenings at the orchestra! For business and client meetings, you can't go wrong with the classic wool coat. Also, select your jewelry carefully. Is it too much or too flashy? Is it too expensive? Depending on your role, costly jewelry may not be appropriate in your work environment. Even worse, it may cause your clients to resent you. Avoid displaying any jewelry, other than traditional earrings, that involves body piercing. Body piercing may be growing more common in everyday life, but it still isn't acceptable in the business world. It's your choice, but it's a risky one. Always check your company's policies.

Never forget to do a last minute, full-body mirror check before going to work in the morning. One person I know could have avoided the humiliation she experienced after an important sales meeting. She looked at herself in the ladies' room mirror, only to realize that you could see through her white skirt! Her red bikini underpants weren't what this woman wanted people focusing on during her sales presentation, and certainly not what she wanted them to remember.

Periodically check yourself during the day, too, to ensure there's no lipstick on your teeth, no runs in your stockings, no hair in your face, etc.

Remember, business travel, off-site meetings, corporate parties, etc., are still part of the professional arena. I have been called in to coach people about proper attire at these functions. In case you are wondering, the bikini doesn't cut it! Nor does a very revealing dress at a holiday party. If you are playing a sport at a company event, find out what you should wear. Country clubs and golf courses usually have strict dress requirements.

Pick and choose the type of company that you want to work for. Is there a dress code? Is the image one you are comfortable with? If not, find someplace else to work. There is no point in working hard only to have your progress stopped because you won't wear the "uniform."

Develop a style that fits you and your company culture well.

Keep in mind that, when it comes to appearance, women are often judged more harshly in the business world than men.

"Women are judged on their appearance first," said Dr. Catherine E. Palmier, Chief Medical Officer of United Healthcare of Georgia.

Pay attention to details

Your visual appearance isn't just about what you wear on your body. It's also about how you take care of your body. Good grooming is an essential part of your exterior packaging. When you value yourself and respect others, when you are motivated to be both approachable and respected, you will pay attention to the details of grooming. In fact, attention to detail is what grooming is all about. Like other aspects of your manner, this requires scrutiny on your part and feedback from others. Check yourself out and ask someone close to you to do so, too. Is there anything about your grooming that could turn people off and, therefore, limit your opportunity for further advancement?

Makeup

The reality is that most women would benefit from a little makeup. As women get older, they need to make changes in the way they apply their makeup. Younger women can sometimes present an attractive appearance with no makeup at all. If they choose to apply makeup, they can use products like eyeliner and mascara moderately. As women get older, however, we need to develop different skills for applying makeup and use certain products (especially eye shadow) even more moderately.

The goal isn't to look like Barbie, but to enhance your natural beauty. Too much makeup can be distracting and send the wrong message. Go to a makeup counter in a major department store and ask the person to help you select items for a "natural" look, or seek the advice of an image consultant.

Hair

Your hair needs to be clean, so wash it regularly. It must also be dandruff-free. If you see any sign of dandruff, take action to get rid of it. There are products on the market that really work. Your hair should also look healthy, not over-processed or teased. Always keep your hair out of your face — and don't play with it!

Hairstyles can be quite controversial. Don't wait for your colleagues to give you unsolicited feedback about your hair. If your hair is offensive or unattractive, people will find it difficult to approach you with negative feedback. Ask someone close to you for an objective opinion. As with all feedback, don't be angry when given constructive criticism. Think about it and look for ways to improve your hairstyle or condition.

Women often ask me if they should cut their hair. The answer is, "It depends." I have heard a number of examples of career women who, once they cut their hair, were seen as more professional. One woman had been given the feedback to cut her hair and had for years laughed it off. Finally, she had it cut. It was only then that she got promoted. She made no other change — just a hair cut.

Hair length became an unexpected issue for one of my own staff members after she co-facilitated a presentation skills training program with me. She is young, attractive, and was dressed appropriately for the session in a conservative navy blue suit. Her blond hair was long and flowing. After the session, the manager informed me that I should never send this young woman to facilitate a session at that company again. The problem? The length of her hair. Although I was surprised, I gave my employee the feedback, and she asked me whether I thought she should cut her hair. I left the decision up to her. She decided that in the future she would be more conscious of keeping her hair pulled back.

Although I disagreed with the client's assessment, I was grateful that she gave me the feedback. It was our choice whether to change and keep the client. Usually, there is no feedback, hence no opportunity to change.

Look at your senior management. Are many (if any) wearing their hair beyond shoulder length? Could this be holding you back? What is the image you're sending? If you decide to wear your hair shorter, choose an appropriate style. The short, punk look could create an image that won't be taken seriously.

Women don't have to have the same look within their work environment. But make decisions carefully. Is having the hairstyle you want worth the risk of not getting the recognition you want even more — and worked so hard to deserve?

Nails

Whether you get a professional manicure, or do your own nails at home, make sure that they are clean, trimmed well and that the polish isn't chipped. Color of polish and length of nails are a personal choice. What works best in your environment? Are your nails a distraction to noting your capabilities? Do they interfere with your ability to do your job? Do they leave polish marks on important papers? If so, make the necessary changes. And, if your toes ever do show, consider getting a pedicure — especially if your office allows sandals and the more casual, open-toe look for shoes.

Teeth

There are three things to keep in mind when it comes to your teeth:

- Make sure that your teeth are straight. If you need adult braces, they are readily available.

- Make sure they are clean. Always check after snacks and meals to ensure nothing is caught between your teeth. Keep dental floss in your office or briefcase and do a spot check in the bathroom mirror after you eat.

- Make sure they are white. See your dentist about a good tooth whitener if you need help in this department.

Ensuring all three teeth-related conditions are met, can help ensure that your smile is as attractive as possible — like the rest of your package.

Tattoos & body piercings

Visible tattoos and body piercings are still not acceptable in most work environments when you're striving for career advancement. This may change in another 10 to 15 years. But you certainly won't look like senior management material today if you show this side of your creative self. It's a risky fashion statement, and may conflict with your company's policies.

Don't sweat it

Sometimes you have to act and look more confident than you actually feel. This can be a problem if your

What you don't see ...

General body odors are a major grooming-related complaint.
I am often asked for advice on how to deal with this issue. If
people are offended by the smells that emanate from your
body, they won't want to work with you. What types of
smells am I talking about? There are four main areas:

- **Perfume** — After you get used to the scent, you often don't
  smell it yourself. Hence, you tend to put on way too much.
  Hint: If people are complimenting you on the scent at 3
  P.M., it was too heavy at 9 in the morning!

- **Smoke** — Nonsmokers are offended by the smell. Remember, cigarette smoking not only gives you bad breath; the
  smell clings to your hair and clothing long after you've had a
  cigarette. If you must smoke, try waiting until the end of the
  day. Better yet, get motivated and quit! You will smell
  better, look better and your body will be healthier.

- **Specific body-oriented smells** — In U.S. culture, it is
  important to bathe or shower daily and use a good deodor-
  ant. Some people have a condition that creates excess body
  odor, but this is rare. If you have it, see a doctor. Specific
  foods also can create bad body odors. These smells linger on
  your clothes and breath, and also come out through your
  pores and sweat. If you eat a lot of garlic and ethnic foods, or
  foods that are different from what your coworkers eat —
  you might want to get some feedback from them. I hear a lot
  of complaints from my clients about their colleague's
  food-related odors.

- **Breath** — Onions, garlic and milk products create bad
  breath. Avoiding them when working is the best bet. You
  can also use mouthwash, breath mints and Breath Assure.

perspiration kicks into high gear when you are nervous.
See a doctor if necessary, try different anti-perspirants or
underarm protectors. If your perspiration is triggered by
nervousness, you may be able to conceal the problem by
wearing loose, layered clothing on days when you have
important presentations. You want people to remember
you as calm, cool and collected, not sweating bullets.

Get physically fit

A physically fit person looks energetic and attractive.
She also looks capable of getting the job done. That's how
other people see you when you take care of the physical
needs and condition of your body. Even more
importantly, when you eat nutritiously, get sufficient
sleep and exercise regularly, you will feel better and, when
you look in the mirror, you will like what *you* see. See your
doctor, join a health club, lose the extra weight. Your good
health is undoubtedly your most important investment.
The payoff is feeling better, looking better, and being a
more productive, capable individual.

What Does Your Body Language Say?

Another important aspect of your visual manner is
your body language. Your professional presence is
affected by your body movements, eye contact and the
way you carry yourself. People interpret your body
language and assume it is an expression of your

confidence and internal values. And they are right! Therefore, be conscious of the image you present through your body language.

Use proper posture.

The proper posture is to stand or sit straight. Try to fill your space regardless of your height. Whenever possible, arrive early to meetings, and if the chair is adjustable, crank it up so you look taller. Women often take too little space around a table during meetings. Keep your hands on the table, not in your lap, and fill your space — don't pull in. Sit erect — no slouching.

Use proper posture to look sure of yourself. Let your self-worth shine through! Unfortunately, I have seen many women slump — particularly tall women. When people stand straight, they appear to be more confident. If you look confident, people will treat you with more respect.

Make eye contact.

Look people in the eye without staring at them. If you look down or away, it indicates a lack of self-assurance or trustworthiness. Your goal isn't to intimidate others, but not be intimidated by them, either.

Smile.

A smile is often friendly, but women need to be careful that they aren't over-smiling. Smiling is often used to hide nervousness. If the smile isn't congruent to the message, a person can look insipid. A smile is appropriate when it is genuine. It can make people feel comfortable. A scowl and sour or stern face can be off-putting.

Look at yourself in the mirror when you are on the phone. What is your face saying about you?

Keep your head straight.

Women tend to tilt their heads to one side. This lacks power. Note female TV broadcasters. They hold their heads straight, naturally centered between their shoulders. Also note that they keep their chins up. When the head tilts down, the look is more acquiescent and deferential. The chin held up conveys more confidence.

Watch the ways you gesture.

It's fine to gesture, as long as your movements match your message and are used sparingly. When the hands are flying out of control, people will judge you as emotional. The larger the group to whom you are speaking, the larger your gestures can — and should — be. Women tend to keep their arms close to their bodies or fold their arms in front of themselves. This creates a small, closed look. The goal is to look large (fill your space) and be expansive. If you don't look "important," how important are your ideas?

Keep nervous habits under control.

There are grooming-related behaviors and habits that women should be careful to avoid. They make you look nervous or insecure. These habits can also be annoying and distracting to others.

- **Playing with hair**. Keep your hands away from your hair. That means no flipping, pushing or twirling.
- **Playing with fingernails**. Please, no biting, picking or cleaning them.
- **Doing personal grooming in public**. Ladies, no hair brushing, powdering, or lipstick application. These activities are best done at home or in the ladies' room.

Walk the walk!

Do you want to swagger? Saunter? Shuffle? No. You want to walk purposefully. Don't tiptoe around like you want to hide. When you walk with purpose, you walk quickly — like you have something to do. That's how others will see you.

Your Vocal Manner

What do others hear?

After reading and considering all the information about clothing, grooming and body language, think about another important aspect of your manner — your voice. The way you sound is an essential part of your professional presence. Your voice creates an image. People frequently will judge you based on how you sound — not just what you say. Often, because telephones are an important part of how we communicate in our jobs, your voice is the first impression people have of you. It's not unusual to do business with some individuals exclusively over the phone. If you never meet face-to-face, the sound of your voice helps them form a mental picture of you. Make it a good one!

I know of many examples where women weren't hired for a position that required a great deal of phone time. If they sounded too squeaky (high pitch), or too nasal (often regional dialects), they would not represent the organization in the most professional manner. Did these people get feedback? Of course not! They simply didn't get the jobs. They didn't know that they needed to improve the way they sounded.

Have you ever been impressed with how someone looks, then she opens her mouth and her voice is high and squeaky? Have you ever felt your eyes glaze over during a presentation because the speaker's voice was totally monotone? How we say what we say creates impact and is definitely part of our manner.

Many women have the incorrect idea that they should speak softly and be deferential to male colleagues. With that attitude, you won't be heard, and you won't project an image of authority.

"You need to speak in a way that will get people to listen," said Debra Brown-Spruill, Executive Director of OCLC — Public Affairs Information Services. Her career has encompassed television reporting, teaching, nursing and modeling. "You have to present yourself in a way that people will take you seriously, that says, 'I belong here and I'm someone to be reckoned with.'" Brown-Spruill took acting lessons which helped improve her speaking voice. She said the best piece of advice she ever got about one's manner was from another woman, who said, "Look around this table. Do you really think that all these people know what they're talking about? Some do, some don't. Just say it with authority."

According to Sue Rusch, a business coach and speaker to direct selling entrepreneurs, "a firmer and louder voice expresses confidence."

Successful women agree that the sound of your voice is important to achieving credibility and authority, and it's worth the time and effort it takes to improve the way you naturally sound. Listen to your voice-mail greeting. Do you sound like someone who is sensible, knowledgeable and authoritative? If not, what do you

need to do to improve? There are eight aspects of your
voice that you should pay attention to:

- **Pitch:** Is your voice high- or low-pitched? A
  high-pitched, squeaky voice sounds like a little girl
  is speaking. That's not the image you want to
  project. Your voice may also get higher pitched
  when you are nervous. This is a natural reaction,
  but it's something you should try to control. It's
  usually not in your best interests to let others know
  you're feeling less than confident. It may also
  sound like you are whining, which annoys most
  listeners. Practice keeping the pitch at low to
  moderate levels. A deeper pitched voice has more
  credibility. If you get nervous when speaking,
  remember to breathe and control your pitch.
  Speak from your diaphragm, not your chest.

- **Volume:** Do you speak too loudly or too softly?
  Although it's never appropriate to yell, having a
  soft voice often makes people sound like they lack
  confidence. Are you projecting enough? If people
  are continually saying, "What did you say?" or
  "Speak up," that's a hint. Get in the habit of
  projecting your voice better. Your volume should
  get people to listen.

- **Rate:** Do you speak too fast or too slow? This
  aspect of speaking has geographical
  considerations. In some regions of the country, if

you are speaking too quickly, you can be thought of as abrasive or rude. If you are too slow, you can be seen as stupid or lazy. Get some feedback: Is your rate appropriate for the people with whom you are speaking? If people are asking you to slow down, or if they are cutting you off or "shushing" you, chances are you need to adjust your tempo.

- **Pause:** Are your pauses in speech effective, or distracting? A silent pause can be very effective. It gives people a chance to think. The pauses can't be too long, or you may appear to be "ponderous." Think of appropriate pause time as punctuation — a one-second pause is like a comma, two seconds is like a semicolon, and three seconds is a period. If you fill your pause time with an "Uh," "Um" or "You know," however, you sound hesitant and your message loses credibility. Start paying more attention to this aspect of your speech. Be sure to pause (be silent briefly) when there is punctuation, then continue to speak. Believe it or not, having direct eye contact with your listener or audience members can help get rid of problems you may have with vocal hesitation. Get a good friend to point out every time you say, "You know." This person can respond by saying, "No, I don't know," or "OK." With attention and feedback, this problem can be eliminated.

- **Rising intonation:** Have you noticed how many women raise their voices at the end of a sentence? It's OK when you are asking a question, but it totally lacks authority when no question is intended. It sounds like a little girl asking for permission. At the end of a sentence, maintain your volume, but drop the pitch. It has more authority.

- **Variety:** Does your voice have expression and variety, or does it sound flat? A flat, monotone voice lacks energy. It is important to show passion and enthusiasm when presenting your ideas. The more "wow" you can create, the more people will listen to what you have to say. It's amazing what a little conviction in your voice can do to sell an idea. Of course, make sure that you are emphasizing the right word. You can take one sentence and emphasize each word differently to create different meanings. Give it a try:
  - **"I** deserve to be recognized."
  - "I **deserve** to be recognized."
  - "I deserve to **be** recognized."
  - "I deserve to be **recognized.**"

- **Foreign accents:** I have worked with many people whose second language is English. Unfortunately, many speak too quickly, and too softly. The goal is to slow down and project. If people have trouble understanding your English, and this is holding you back from speaking up and being noticed, it's time to get some coaching for accent reduction.

- **Regional accents:** Depending on where you are located in the country, a regional accent can negatively affect the impression you have on others. It is possible to reduce (or even change) your accent if it becomes an impediment. Consult with a vocal coach.

Your Verbal Manner

What you say counts

You might wonder if the words you use also count. They most certainly do! They have a huge impact on the initial impressions we make.

"People need to be aware that everything they communicate will make an impact," said Christine James-Brown, President & CEO of United Way of Southeastern Pennsylvania. "It forms an overall composite of you. Informal communication is critically important. What you say or don't say on an elevator — people pay attention to it. You need to be aware of who you communicate with and how. Act as if you are empowered."

I recall an experience I had following a presentation given at a regional sales meeting. At lunch, I noticed people wearing award ribbons on their suits. I asked a man standing near me in the buffet line why he was wearing the ribbon. He said, "I won this award last night. I worked hard for it. I'm really excited and proud to get it." As I continued through the buffet line, I saw a woman wearing a similar ribbon and I asked her why she received it. She said, "Last night, we had an awards banquet. I got lucky. I couldn't have done it without help from others."

This experience is a telling example of how men take ownership of their accomplishments and women give the credit away. If you discount your hard work by saying you don't deserve the recognition you receive, people will probably believe you. When you get recognition for your efforts, *own it*!

Avoid power robbers

Power robbers are words that rob you of your personal power. This includes words like: "I guess," "I hope," "I think," "maybe," "sorta," "kinda," and "probably." These words tell your listener you are not sure about what you are saying. Try not to use them.

Sue Rusch, a business coach and speaker to direct selling entrepreneurs, agrees. "Avoid 'yea,' 'uh huh,' and tentative language like 'I think' and 'I believe,' which can create a perception of insincerity," she said.

For example, what would your reaction be if I said:

- I **guess** you will be helped by reading this book.
- I **hope** you will be helped by reading this book.
- I **think** you will be helped by reading this book.

- I **believe** you will be helped by reading this book.
- You **will be** helped by reading this book.

Would you read this book if I only guessed it would help you? Probably not. In fact, if I was unsure that it would help my readers, I wouldn't even be motivated to write it!

There are times when you can't commit, and you should be honest about it. But be careful not to give a wishy-washy impression in the long run.

Don't minimize your ideas by prefacing them with put-downs. Many women have a tendency to present ideas in this way:

"This may not work, but I think we could … "
"I have an idea. You might not like it because … "
"Do you think there's a way to … "
"I'm sorry, I was just wondering if … "

If you don't have confidence in your ideas and opinions, your colleagues won't, either. Stop saying you're sorry! Stop putting your ideas and contributions down. Believe in yourself and your abilities. Choose words that make people listen and believe in you.

Your verbal manner counts even more once people have adjusted to your visual image and the way you use your voice.

Other verbal "no-no's"

Be conscious of the following ways your verbal manner can detract from your professional image:

- **Swearing:** As bad as it is for men to use vulgarities, women tend to be judged even more harshly. Why risk offending people? Do not swear. What words are people sensitive to? I know of one situation where a speaker wasn't invited back because she said, "Oh my God." To that audience, the speaker's choice of words was offensive. Respect yourself and others. Use words that dignify you and your role, not detract from it. "Don't swear. I used to, and people didn't want to deal with me," said Judith C. Giordan, Ph.D., a former executive and corporate officer at several *Fortune* 500 companies.

- **Jargon and acronyms:** There are times when using buzzwords, jargon and acronyms is accepted and even expected. But if everyone you talk to doesn't understand what you are saying, you run the risk of excluding people. Professionals who are successful self-marketers know when to use jargon and acronyms, and when not to. If you are not sure, check with the person to whom you are speaking. If he or she doesn't know the terms, be flexible and use words or explanations that are more clear.

- **Pretentious language:** When speaking, use words that the other person understands. Even if you are using the proper word, if it intimidates others, it isn't the proper choice. Having a large vocabulary is a wonderful thing. I encourage you to expand yours through reading. However, only use those bigger, less familiar words when appropriate. People won't promote you or be your advocates if you make them feel stupid.

- **Compliments:** Give them! And, when you receive a compliment, just say, "Thank you." Accept compliments graciously. By doing so, you are telling the person who complimented you that you appreciate his or her opinion and you value it. Refusing to accept a compliment because you want to be humble can make the other person uncomfortable. It also sends a message that you don't value yourself enough. Even worse, if you tell other people you don't deserve the compliment, they may believe you! They may hesitate to recognize your contributions in the future.

"My attitude of 'Don't stand out, be humble,' hindered me," Craun said. She says her presence has evolved over the years, and her manner now is "a quiet confidence" that has helped, not hindered her career.

If you deserve the compliment, accept it. Remember that "Thank you" is the polite response, not "No problem." Make sure you recognize the accomplishments of others, too.

Add an "s" to "Manner" and You Have "Manners" Your Manners Matter!

Manner is a lot more than skin deep. In my executive coaching practice, I am often asked to speak on business etiquette. How you behave professionally is, in my experience and that of the women I have interviewed, a career maker or breaker. Get it right. You may look the part, but if you don't act it, you won't go very far.

Common courtesies count!

A telling consequence of bad business etiquette: The Research Institute of America reported that 96 percent of customers never complain about discourteous professionals, but 91 percent specifically decide *not to do business with companies who have in some way offended them.*

No corporate giant is going to risk its reputation because of your bad manners.

It is essential that you pay attention to common courtesies. They make a difference in the relationships we create and the impressions we make.

The basics of good manners

These simple courtesies sound so obvious, but I can't tell you how many people take them for granted. Remember to:

- Say "please" and "thank you," "hello" and "goodbye."
- Smile and look interested in others … and listen.
- Open doors for others, regardless of gender.
- Look at people when you talk to them.
- Introduce yourself and others.
- Be helpful.
- Respect people's time.
- Compliment people.
- Write thank-you notes.
- Do what you say you will do.

Technology

A man giving a presentation actually stopped everything to take a call on his cell phone. The entire audience was forced to wait while he responded to the caller and held a conversation that definitely could have waited until later. I was there; I saw and heard the whole thing, and from the reactions of the audience members, I knew that they were not pleased at this display of rudeness. Never make the same mistake. While modern technology has changed the way we do business, it has not lowered the standards of courteous behavior. In fact, it opens up a new area in which you are expected to mind your manner(s). Follow these guidelines:

- **Cell phones:** Cell phones shouldn't be used in public areas, and should be turned off during meetings and presentations. Never disrupt the service you are performing to take a call on your cell phone *or* regular phone.

- **Pagers/beepers:** Put them on vibrate.

- **E-mail:** Check your spelling, keep it short, and always use a subject line. Be careful what you write — this is not a private form of communication.

- **Fax:** When faxing to hotels, "white out" client names and confidential information.

- **Speaker phone:** Don't use it unless it's a conference call; people who don't pick up their phones are seen as arrogant.

- **Voice mail:** Keep your own voice-mail greeting short and change it regularly so people know how to reach you. When you leave a message on someone else's voice mail, say your name and phone number slowly at the beginning and end of the message.

- **Telephone:** Put a smile on your face and nothing in your mouth — no gum, mints or food. Also remember, no one likes to be put on hold.

Meeting manners

Be sure you plan and conduct meetings with court-eous attention to details. People will remember your consideration. Here are the manners *you* should remember:

- Be very specific when scheduling a meeting. Double check dates and times. Also, verify all appointments at least 48 hours in advance.

- Make sure the equipment works and that there is backup if something goes wrong.

- Do not have sidebar conversations.

- Be prepared. Have the right information.

- Turn off cell phones; put pagers on vibrate.

- Follow through with what you promised.

Take the time to demonstrate common courtesy in all of your interactions. It's good for your career, and it's simply the right thing to do.

"What you see is an outward professionalism, but there is an inward kindness, caring and reflectiveness," Rusch said.

Remember to treat others with respect and courtesy, and they will remember you!

The Behavior Balancing Act

Your behavior reflects your manners. Fine-tuning your professional behavior is a balancing act. You know you can't sit back and expect to get noticed. You can't be a pushover. But you don't want to get a reputation for being a diva, either. People won't want to be around you if you get in their faces, show off, or act like the universe revolves around you. You must be prepared to deal with a wide variety of personalities and situations, knowing when to assert yourself and when to let the other person make a point.

Know when to speak out — and then do it

Women typically find they not only have to work harder than men; they have to be more careful about the image they present. Many women refrain from speaking out because they are reluctant to rock the boat. They may have a natural tendency to be deferential to men. Successful women recognize the need to be outspoken, but they choose their battles carefully.

"I am sometimes hindered because I value harmony so much that I don't like to make waves," said Lynn A. Tetrault, Vice President Human Resources at AstraZeneca.

"Occasionally, I will refrain from bringing things up and will compromise." It has been her experience that a woman who gets argumentative and uses an aggressive tone risks being labeled a "bitch." Tetrault does set boundaries, however. For example, she will never compromise on ethics.

"Unfortunately, you still have to expect inequities," said Giordan. "But know who you are and what you will tolerate." She tries to find finds ways to express herself without coming across as harsh. "You need to say things in a way that you will be heard. You want to pull instead of push," she said. You can disagree without being ignored or discounted. For example, Giordan suggests telling the other person, "That was an excellent idea. Do you mind if I build on it?" Or, if you think someone is incorrect, she suggests you say, "I haven't seen it like that," or another equally balanced statement, but then say what you do believe.

"Women need to use language that doesn't discount their thoughts, but that also allows them to be heard, and isn't perceived as coming across as aggressive," said Giordan. "An approach like 'Building on what you said, I think … ' strikes a good balance. You make your point while recognizing the contribution of the other person."

Speaking at inopportune times can be damaging. What happens when women are too outspoken? "They are seen as threats," said Aida Levitan, Ph.D., CEO of Publicis Sanchez and Levitan, "and then people are prejudiced against you."

Although I never advocate being rude, I do believe there are times when you need to bend the rules. If everyone at a meeting is interrupting, don't wait for your turn. You won't get one. In that atmosphere, no one is going to say, "Sally, we haven't heard from you in a while. What is your opinion?" If the work culture is one where it's acceptable to jump in, then jump in!

"Things like politeness, waiting my turn to speak out at meetings, got in my way of expressing thoughts in public settings," Craun said. "Now, if I need to interrupt, I will."

As a rule of thumb, you should speak up within the first 10 minutes of a meeting in order to get yourself established as a contributor. If you wait any longer, you risk being overlooked as a member of the group. You will also find it becomes more difficult to start participating the longer you wait. If there are only a few women at a meeting, sit separately to avoid the appearance of being a "girls' club."

Treat everyone right

Malcolm Forbes once said, "There are no unimportant people." Remember this in all your professional interactions. Your good manners will make your coworkers and employers feel important. It will show that you value them and their role in the company.

Try to do what is right and fair for the company and the people with whom you work, and you will be known as a person of integrity. Do not cause other employees to be emotional casualties of your mistakes or aggressive style.

Take responsibility. If your performance was lacking in some way, 'fess up. We all make mistakes. Admit it, propose a remedy and initiate damage control.

Do not take credit for other people's work. Give credit where credit is due. However, don't discount your contribution. I have seen many women get lost in the team. It is critical to be accountable for what you've done. That includes getting recognized when you succeed!

Stay away from gossip. Avoid gossipers. Talking negatively about others and participating in the rumor mill will never make you look good.

Follow the advice of Sue Rusch, the business coach and speaker to direct selling entrepreneurs. She recommends courtesies like sending thank-you notes and returning phone calls promptly. Don't let people feel left out of conversations and meetings. Introduce and include them. "Successful women know that it's the small 1% steps that lead to 100% success," Rusch said.

Be mature

Avoid overly emotional reactions in the workplace. These behaviors will hinder your career and make you seem immature:

- Giggling: This typically indicates nervousness and makes you look silly.

- Crying: When it happens, it usually makes others feel uncomfortable. Prepare for difficult conversations by role-playing. Remember to breathe. If you feel tears starting to well up in your eyes, excuse yourself from the meeting, if possible. If not, bring out the tissue, breathe, and keep going.

"Competent women need to come off as confident women, ladylike but not strident," said Jeanie Duck, author of the book *Change Monster: The Human Forces that Fuel or Foil Corporate Transformation and Change*, and Senior Vice President of The Boston Consulting Group.

Dealing with difficult people

It's inevitable that you will have to deal with difficult people: crazy bosses, backstabbing coworkers, and immature trainees. My best advice is to keep the lines of communication open. When people stop communicating, battle lines are drawn and there is likely to be fallout. At the very least, an emotionally charged workplace creates stress and reduces productivity. The worst case scenario is that careers can be damaged or destroyed.

Be discerning. Take whatever steps you can to address issues before they blow up. But know when to back off and protect your own career.

Be a good listener

Make your point, but also be a good listener. Peggie Pelosi-Gardiner, Vice President of Network Development for USANA Health Sciences, said she has been told that she has the ability "to make others feel like they are the

---

Do's & Don'ts of Listening

Do
- Paraphrase the speaker to indicate understanding
- Make empathy-based statements
- Ask appropriate and relevant questions
- Make statements that keep conversation flowing

Don't
- Interrupt
- Switch subjects midstream
- Tune out and daydream
- Finish sentences for other people

---

only people in the room." Pelosi-Gardiner listens with intent, using eye contact, the other person's name and really focusing on that person. She calls this "a caring dialogue."

Create your own opportunities to have caring dialogues. People will seek you out because you are interested in them.

Keep it private

Be careful where you hold conversations. The information highway isn't just modern technology. The old-fashioned rumor mill is still up and running!

News travels fast, whether it's overheard in elevators, hallways, public transportation, restaurants or airlines. You may not even be aware that people are listening. The people who overhear you may know the people about whom you are speaking, or know someone who knows someone. As you may already know from experience, it can get ugly fast.

So, watch what you say, and *where* you say it.

Be positive

Develop a reputation for having a positive manner about your business and the people you work with. "Feeling good about yourself exudes confidence and creates an energy in the room," said Michelle A. Rosen, Senior Director Strategy, Business Development at

McDonald's Corp. "People don't want to be around naysayers."

"Have a positive attitude," said Peggi Einhorn, Senior Vice President of JPMorganChase. "You need to have a positive attitude for leadership and be enthusiastic."

With your manner — and your manners — under control, there's no limit to what you can achieve.

Chapter 3 ~ A

Advocates: Add Their Influence to Your Marketing Plan

"I t's not just who you know, but who knows you and what you are capable of doing that truly matters."

I repeat this statement countless times to the hundreds of audiences I have spoken to about the critical importance of having advocates to advance your career. During executive coaching sessions, as well, especially with my female clients, the issue of advocacy takes top priority.

That's why the **A** in my **MAGIC** marketing plan is devoted to advocacy. It's important to understand what advocates are and are not, and why developing advocates is such a vital part of anyone's self-marketing plan. This chapter is all about increasing your awareness of the advocates around you and understanding how to appropriately cultivate those relationships.

In this chapter I will share stories and advice from successful women who know first hand about the value of creating advocates. You will also find exercises designed to help you create a plan of action for strengthening the support of key individuals in your life. Give extra attention to the information you find in the following pages. It is guaranteed to help you get the opportunities and recognition you need to realize your goals.

A wise family friend once told me, "People are generally successful to the degree others want them to be successful." So read on. It's time to build your team of people who are invested in and rooting for your success!

So, Just What Is an Advocate?

An advocate as defined by the dictionary is "one who pleads another's cause." My definition is a bit broader. I believe that advocates are those individuals who are willing either from direct exposure or benefit, to speak out in support of your abilities, your character and your value. Their opinions are given in terms of what they believe you have to offer individuals, groups or an organization. An advocate is your champion — someone who sells you and sells for you.

Advocates come in all colors, shapes, sizes and yes, even job titles. Too many people make the mistake of thinking that the only advocate they need to be concerned about is their immediate manager or someone else in a position of authority. While the relationship you have with management-types is essential to your standing in a company, don't overlook the need for and importance of other people's opinion of you. Virtually anyone you work with and know has the potential to be your advocate.

Start With the Person You Report To

While your manager cannot — and should not — be your only advocate, let's spend a moment on how to make that relationship as strong and mutually beneficial as possible.

One of the first senior executives I ever coached shared with me that his expectation of all of his subordinates was that their number one priority was to make him look good. Now that may sound egotistical at first glance, but think about it: In order for managers at any level to be effective, they must count on the people reporting to them to do their jobs effectively and efficiently. Make sure that you are someone your manager can trust to deliver, and deliver well. Also, never compromise your manager by not keeping him or her informed or going over his or her head. In most cases, this loyalty will in turn be rewarded by loyalty.

Another way to gain support from your manager is to be the person who "takes things off his or her desk" vs. being someone who constantly "puts stuff on it." What this means: Consider all of the responsibilities and priorities your boss has as a collection of file folders covering the desk, then decide whether you help make the situation simpler or more complicated.

The more successful you help your manager to be, the stronger he or she will be as your advocate. This happens on two fronts: The first comes from his or her support of you out of gratitude and a desire to return the favor. The second comes when your manager's success puts him or her in a more influential position within your organization.

Unfortunately, not all managers have your best interest at heart or are willing to put your development and promotion before their own personal agenda. What should you do if you find yourself in this position? Several of the women I spoke with agreed: If you find yourself with an unsupportive manager, get a new one. Look for other opportunities within the company to work for someone who will appreciate your efforts and talent, and who genuinely will be willing to advance your career pursuits not just his or her own.

Move Beyond Your Manager as an Advocate

When it comes to a group of decision makers weighing in on who may get the next promotion or highly sought after assignment, many will expect your manager to be your advocate. They are likely to see his or her support as a "given." That's because it would reflect poorly back on your manager to have anyone but a top performer on his or her team.

Therefore, you need to make sure that individuals with the same degree of authority and/or influence also appreciate what you have to offer. If you consider your manager as a *primary advocate*, these individuals could be termed as your *secondary advocates*. Building a network of secondary advocates is essential.

Advocates: Add Their Influence to Your Marketing Plan

Many of the executive women I spoke with said that they went out of their way to take on projects that put them in front of key people. They called these assignments "high risk and reward projects."

The strong visibility that came with these initiatives left them open to exposure if they failed, but gave them significant positive attention when they succeeded. These projects also brought them into the field of view of many who might otherwise never have truly known or appreciated their capabilities. As Janice Price, President and CEO of The Kimmel Center for the Performing Arts in Philadelphia, put it: "You can't request advocates; you need to earn them."

Susan Ward, a Vice President of UPS, sees it this way: "If your work isn't visible and the position and people you work with don't have visibility, find a way out. You need to be in high profile places."

Looking "up" in an organization is only one place to find and cultivate your network of *secondary advocates*. Truly successful people respect and connect with peers, subordinates and individuals at all levels in their company.

Cheryl Doll, Vice President of Marketing at LodgeWorks, was quick to point out: "Advocates don't have to have titles. There are some people who are in the know and are connected but they don't have executive positions." An in-house travel agent, for example, became an unexpected advocate. This travel agent noticed that Doll was careful about spending company money when traveling for business. For example, she made it a habit to stay at her parents' house when working at corporate headquarters. The travel agent told Doll's manager that she was a team player who was conscientious about saving the company money. "The best advocates are not always people in power," Doll concluded.

The former Executive Vice President of CNN News Group, Gail Evans, said, "I have had as many advocates working for me as I have had who were my boss." She added, "My greatest advocates were women who worked for me. They had accolades about me because I took care of them. People who worked for me felt cared for and taken care of, even when they disagreed with my decisions. I promoted people who became my advocates." Evans, author of the book *She Wins, You Win*, also said, "You should try to develop a reputation as someone who is good to work for."

Building Your Advocate Network — Serendipity or Strategy?

So, is having a strong group of advocates an act of chance or determination? The answer is both. To truly expand the base of people who "know you and what you are capable of doing," you must be prepared to make the most of opportunities and people who come into your life. You must also take the initiative to bring a few key people in on your own.

Advocates: Add Their Influence to Your Marketing Plan

As I've already discussed, existing and potential advocates likely surround you. The objective is to take stock of who they are, and how you can strengthen their understanding of your capabilities and overall perception.

Many, if not most, of these individuals have come into your life by chance. For example, you may have inherited your manager or subordinates when you switched departments or started working for your company. Likewise, your colleagues and closest team members came with your overall employment package. Choosing to work with them was not an option, but HOW you choose to work with them is.

Other potential advocates, too, may have been the result of serendipity — a chance encounter in an elevator or working together on a special team project. Community and volunteer work, and social relationships with people who have common interests or work in the same industry, may also develop into advocacy.

For Heidi Hunter, Vice President and Global Business Manager, Oncology at Wyeth, previous advocate relationships were most definitely secured by serendipity. "In the past, they just happened," she stated. "Now, I realize that strategically it's important to actively seek advocates. I do this by asking for their time and making an effort to do things for these people."

Beyond what I touched on earlier about cultivating a good relationship with your manager and key decision makers, seizing advocate opportunities with others requires several things. This list includes some of the most

basic principles of good business behavior and professional presence. It also includes taking the initiative to be
thoughtful, creative and disciplined enough to follow-
through with people. Here are my seven suggestions:

- Make sure that your packaging, your *Manner* as
  we talked about in Chapter 2, reflects well on the
  pride and care you take in having a polished
  professional image.

- Never, and I mean never, underestimate the
  importance of a good handshake. You want it to
  be firm (not bone crushing), thumb "web" to
  "web" (so people get your full hand, not just your
  fingertips), with the right amount of strength that
  reveals confidence, and delivered with direct eye
  contact. Know that a handshake, like business
  etiquette in general, is gender neutral. Be assertive
  when handshaking and set the tone as a person
  who is in control.

- Be prepared with an appropriate self-introduction.
  Beyond just giving your name, consider stating
  your role in a way that also immediately makes
  clear how you contribute to the organization in a
  meaningful way. If you are a customer service
  representative, you might say, "I'm Samantha
  Sullivan. I am a proud member of the customer
  service team that was just rated number one in our
  industry by our National Account Customers."

- Always carry an ample supply of business cards wherever you go. The business card — in good shape and readily available — is an extremely important tool. Even if your company doesn't print cards for you, spend some money and have a calling card printed with your name and personal contact information.

  If you meet someone you want to contact again, ask for his or her card, then offer yours. This way, you can follow up and contact the person. I also like to jot down a note or two on the back of the other person's card — where we met, what we talked about and what I want to do when I return to the office (send articles, follow up with a phone call, etc.). If the person doesn't have a card, use one of yours, cross out your information (ensuring you don't accidentally give someone else the card), and write his or her contact details on the back.

- Establish a reputation of being a person who keeps her word. If you meet someone and promise him or her something such as a follow-up phone call, the name of a contact or the author of a business book you just read — make sure that you deliver on that promise in a timely fashion.

- Be well read about your company and the industry that you are in. This will give you the opportunity to engage in more meaningful conversations and be seen as someone who "understands the big picture."

- Be known as someone who respects others and the value that they bring to a team or corporation — once again, regardless of title or position. I have a friend who once worked with a CEO who formed opinions on the career potential of new middle managers by finding out what the security guards in the lobby thought of them. And believe me, he asked.

Making the most out of serendipitous encounters is only one way to build a powerful network of advocates. It is equally important to take a strategic look at who you should consciously cultivate to be in your pool of champions.

Let's Talk Strategy

In speaking with the group of accomplished women I interviewed for this book, it was interesting to hear the variety of perspectives they brought on the subject of strategically seeking out advocates. While most I spoke with felt that advocates had been integral in their success, many had not realized the necessity of being more strategic in cultivating advocates until later in their careers.

"If only I knew then what I know now about the impact these relationships can have," was a common theme among the women I spoke with. Their universal advice, "Make the time and effort now to surround yourself with people who can help you reach your goals. Otherwise, you may look back some day with questions about what could have been."

"I could have been more strategic early on," sighed Catherine J. Ross, President, Security Services, for Day & Zimmerman in Philadelphia. "But I didn't know how to play the game." Fortunately, she had an advocate step into her life at a past job, a woman who showed Ross the ropes and spoke about her positively to executives. Ross didn't always know some of the people who were her advocates, and initially didn't realize how helpful those advocates were. It took time for her to realize that seeking out advocates and cultivating relationships with them was worth doing strategically. Ross was promoted several times because others recommended her.

Lynn Tetrault, Vice President Human Resources at AstraZeneca, confessed, "I didn't seek out many advocates early in my career. They just happened. My advocates were people who observed my performance or heard about me through others. Once I came to appreciate how much support often comes along through these advocate connections, I started taking a proactive approach to seeking out and developing the relationships. Now I am consciously strategic about getting advocates. I am also more active in supporting other women in my organization, so that I can be advocates for them."

Tetrault also pointed out, "Understand the organization politics and hierarchy. Listen for people who are respected and in strong positions of influence and connect with them at conferences or volunteer to help on something where you will get better exposure."

Sheryl Craun, Vice President of Client Services at ADP Retirement Services, agrees with taking the initiative to develop a network of advocates. She advised, "Target who you want as advocates. One advocate I sought was successful in the type of role I wanted to be in. I observed his characteristics and ultimately called and asked to talk to him about my career. He was open and he gave the advice I use today: 'If you want that next job, act like you are already in it.' He also said, 'Think for yourself, and take each idea down several paths before making a decision.'" She went on to note that this advocate would check in with her to see how things were going; he recommended that she be part of a quality team that became the link to the job she has today.

Aida Levitan, Ph.D., CEO of Publicis Sanchez & Levitan of Miami, put it this way, "You need to identify the key movers and shakers who have influence on your future. Identify and cultivate them." For her career, Levitan felt it was important to cultivate advocates who were media, corporate and civic leaders. She said it was a great experience getting to know these interesting and vital people.

When Serendipity & Strategy Meet

Seizing opportunities is a must for taking optimum advantage of building your advocate relationships. One client shared the following story that truly illustrates this point.

Shirley was in the finance division of a pharmaceutical firm. An avid fitness buff, she worked out in the company gym … every morning except one wonderfully serendipitous day when she had to attend a 7 AM meeting. First, she went to the company cafeteria to grab a cup of coffee. There she saw Tom, who was a division president. They knew each other in passing, but had very limited contact. Shirley recognized this chance encounter as an opportunity that she couldn't pass up.

She purposefully got in line behind Tom. They started a conversation. Tom mentioned that he was in the cafeteria every day at 7 AM. Shirley knew exactly what to do with that information — she changed her workout time to noon, making sure that she was in the cafeteria talking to Tom every morning.

Over time, Shirley developed a good relationship with Tom, and looked for ways to add value to the challenges he was facing in his position. She knew that she needed to be more than just a pleasant conversationalist over coffee. Shirley also made sure that Tom was aware of her capabilities and interests, and sought out his advice from time to time on important matters in her working life.

Just over a year after their first chance encounter, Shirley was promoted to vice president in Tom's division.

As Oprah Winfrey has been credited with saying, **"Luck is when opportunity meets preparation."**

On the following pages, I would like you to take a few minutes to complete an "Advocate Awareness Exercise." This will help you prepare your strategic plan to grow your advocates. By completing this exercise, you can immediately begin to capture your "opportunities."

But before you go to the exercise, I want you try something to get your juices flowing. Here's a little quiz with some role play examples to consider:

Question #1 Let's suppose you are in human resources, but want to move to marketing. Who could be your advocate when it comes to getting recommended or hired for a marketing position?

Answer: Human resources is a great place to find out who key people are within a department. Consider who is head of marketing, what are some of the challenges the department is facing and how your skill set might be a match. Go to lunch with a couple of product managers to start getting exposure.

Question #2 You are an administrative assistant and you want to move into sales. Who would be helpful to have as an advocate?

Answer: Look for projects or ways to increase your interactions with salespeople in the organization. Develop a reputation as someone who is outgoing, confident and not afraid to "dig in." As you come to know people in sales, ask for their advice about what might be the best entry point given your background and experience.

Question #3 You are in sales and want to get customers within a specific industry. Who might be your advocate?

Answer: This may require some homework. Your best advocates are likely to be satisfied customers who will recommend you and the product or service you are selling; people who know firsthand that you are reliable, honest, easy to work with, etc. You should also find out who makes purchasing decisions in the various companies within that industry and connect with them. Frequently, the influencing factor regarding what product or service to purchase and who to purchase it from comes from higher up in an organization. Focus on getting to know their managers, too.

Your Advocate Awareness Exercise

Who are your current advocates:

At Work	In Your Field	In Your Community

Now that you've identified your current advocates, think strategically. Consider your goals.

Who would it help to have as advocates:

At Work	In Your Field	In Your Community

Networking Your Way to Advocates

As you've seen from this exercise, there are two kinds of potential advocates: people you already know and can begin to develop as advocates, and people you haven't even met yet, but know that you certainly should. That's where networking comes in.

So, let's spend a few minutes on those wonderful, interesting and influential people you are soon going to meet! Where do these people hang out? Chances are, not in your cubicle. So how do you find them?

Be proactive and prepared to meet people everywhere you go. As I reviewed earlier, making sure that you have a professional presence, great handshake and a business card with you at all times are a must. Creating opportunities to put that tool kit into practice is also important.

Know where the people you want to meet are going to be. Within your company, meetings, training sessions, the cafeteria, the gym and company-sponsored events are all opportunities to put your networking savvy to the test. Outside of your company, look for ways to attend trade association meetings, industry-related groups, conferences and community events. Staying involved in these activities will put you in contact with a wide array of potential advocates. It will also make you a more interesting person.

"Involvement requires developing relationships and support and seeking feedback from a wide spectrum of colleagues, superiors, industry contacts — people you appreciate and value, and who can contribute to your professional agendas," said Roslyn Courtney, Managing Director of Roslyn Courtney Consulting. Courtney is leading a major initiative to study exemplary women leaders across industries.

Do your homework before a planned networking event or large gathering. Find out who will be there that you might want to connect with. Know facts about them or about something that might interest them — a new development in the organization or industry, a current event that might impact your business, happenings in a country or special place you know they like to visit. Don't ever waste your time at a networking event on the food or drink, or just hanging out with your pals.

"At first I thought networking was not that important," shared Ellen Levine, Editor-in-Chief, *Good Housekeeping*. "But now I know networking is critical in career advancement. Networking helps, it opens doors."

Developing Relationships

Whether advocates have come to you by design or good fortune, it's essential to nurture such relationships. Advocates can evolve over time through your hard work and patience in allowing these contacts to grow. However, rather than just letting them evolve, there are specific things you can do to speed up the process.

Advocates: Add Their Influence to Your Marketing Plan

It doesn't matter whether you have just met your potential advocates or you have known them for some time, there are general methods that will help both types of relationships develop.

With all advocates, create opportunities to have positive interactions as well as purposely choosing assignments and projects with high visibility as we discussed earlier. "Be the obvious choice for the next job and any opportunity," said Jo Anne Rolle Harper, Vice President, Sales Steere Pharmaceuticals at Pfizer Inc. "Your goal is that your face and name pop into their mind. When you deliver performance, you are noticed. People recognize what you do."

McDonald Corp.'s Michelle A. Rosen, Senior Director Strategy, Business Development, advises, "First, be remembered for your accomplishments." She adds, "Another way to interact positively with your colleague is to ask the person for advice. It is a compliment to a person when you ask for their opinion and can make them feel important."

Remember, although it may help your career if you get to know a particular person better, you can also make a difference in your potential advocate's life as well. Look for ways to help others succeed. Use your knowledge and/or experience to offer insight and guidance, especially if you find that your perspective helps broaden a person's understanding or approach to an issue. Focus on what you can do for this person, not necessarily on what he or she can do for you.

It also helps to find out what interests and concerns others. Learn to listen effectively and ask questions. Ask, for example, "What has led to your success?" Or, to start a conversation that gets at the heart of what's on a person's mind, think about asking, "What keeps you up at night?" If you truly listen to the response and then offer your concern, help or suggestions, you may end up sharing experiences and best practices you've encountered that can help your advocate.

Finally, once the relationship gets started, keep it active with quick and simple contacts when more involved ones may not always be feasible. If you know a person has a particular interest in something, for example, look for articles or other bits of relevant information that you can send his or her way with a note.

Judith C. Giordan, Ph.D., former executive and corporate officer at several *Fortune* 500 companies, believes you need to see advocates at least twice a year. "Try to create joint projects, send out holiday and birthday cards. Tell them what you're doing if it will benefit them. Genuinely be concerned about the other person and their business needs. It's what I call 'value-net bonding.'" Giordan added that she believes in a "Pay Forward" not "Pay Back" philosophy with regard to advocates.

Pay attention to your advocates' accomplishments. Acknowledging them with a quick call or card of congratulations will also help keep you connected.

Don't Confuse Advocates With Mentors

Advocates and mentors are not the same thing, so it is important to understand the difference. I will discuss the benefits of finding a mentor in the next chapter in greater detail.

As I noted before, advocates are people who, based on their recommendation, will open doors for you — they sell for you.

A mentor, on the other hand, is someone you have an official or unofficial relationship with whom you speak to get advice on specific areas in which to grow. A mentor is someone you admire because of his or her knowledge, wisdom or position. Learning from this person is the major goal of your mentor relationship.

Mentoring can be equally as rewarding — personally and professionally — as being an advocate. Diana Ruddick, Vice President, Distribution Development & Communications at MassMutual Financial Group, said, "Be a positive influence on people. Coach others. People remember that and your reputation radiates out."

Mentors can become advocates, but advocates aren't necessarily — or even likely — to be your mentor.

A Final Note on Advocacy

Start your advocate quest immediately. Consider the options I have discussed in this chapter. Take stock of who you are, what you have to offer and who you need to help you fulfill your goals and dreams.

Building your network of advocates is a lifelong journey. The people you come to know along the way will not only help you advance your career, they will enrich your life.

Chapter 4 ~ G

Never Stop Growing

If you're not green and growing, you're ripe and rotting. That humorous expression has a profound meaning, and it's not about tomatoes. It's about what you choose to do with your life.

You can take the attitude that your learning days are over; you've proven you are an outstanding worker and your experience is sufficient for achieving any goals. Or, you can look at each day as an opportunity to learn more, try something new, expand your mind and develop your abilities.

It's a choice between growing and reaching your potential, or becoming stagnant, outdated, and eventually obsolete.

The correct choice is obvious — you must grow. Grow is what the "G" stands for in my **MAGIC** formula. It means developing new knowledge, skills and capabilities. Growing is an essential part of your self-marketing plan.

You are already a great worker with a solid performance record. Why is growth a part of self-marketing? Because even if you are at your peak right now — the top of your game — if you keep doing what you're doing the same way you're doing it, you may not be marketable a few years from now, maybe not even in a few months.

Don't be lulled into a false sense of security when it comes to your abilities. While you're in this type of comfort zone, your career could be headed into a dangerous area.

As I've said before, achieving your goals in the business world involves being proactive. In a sense, it's the survival of the fittest — and there is the constant possibility that someone (or some technological advance) will come along to challenge your status. You cannot afford to rest on your laurels.

Our world is constantly changing. Corporations quickly embrace the latest technology; employees are expected to acquire any necessary skills and hit the ground running. Higher education has become more accessible; college degrees are expected, master's degrees are common. If you don't keep yourself informed and educated, you can be sure someone else will come along who does possess the requisite knowledge or skills. That person will get the best projects and opportunities, the promotion you wanted, or maybe even your job.

Keep in mind that if you become a dinosaur, your job could be history. You may think your life is steady and predictable, that you can count on having a job and a fulfilling career based on the knowledge and experience you already possess. But if you fail to keep growing, have an inflexible attitude and consider change to be an unwelcome visitor, you will not be able to compete with workers who are developing new skills, adding to their professional credentials, and adapting fluidly to the ever-changing dynamics of the corporate world.

My advice to grow, therefore, comes with a sense of urgency. Growing also has advantages that extend beyond your job security. Growth draws you closer to reaching your potential. It enables you to learn new things, leads you to new places, and introduces you to new people. Life is more interesting and exciting when you look at the world with a desire and willingness to grow.

When you pursue growth in knowledge and skills, you have more to contribute to your business networks and advocate relationships. You develop an ability to listen more intently and observe more keenly. People respond to you positively because they sense your interest and enthusiasm. They enjoy having conversations with you, and want to be around you. They also see your effort and respect that you try to grow.

This commitment to growth can set you apart. It gives your life more meaning and purpose.

"Everything I do is about learning," said Molly D. Shepard, President and CEO, The Leader's Edge. "I learn from every meeting, every conversation, everything I read. I learn daily."

Resolve to wake up each day with the thought in your head that there is a world of knowledge and opportunity awaiting you. Ask yourself, "What can I do to grow today?" then get up and get to it! Make it a rule that your day is not complete unless you have done something you never did before, or learned something new.

This is not to say, however, that it's sufficient to learn "factoids" and other useless topics best left as trivia quiz answers. Know *what* you should be learning to achieve your goals and reach your potential. Know *why* you are learning, so your efforts are focused.

Can you afford to ever stop growing? The answer is absolutely, positively, no.

When it comes to growth, you can learn a lesson from trees. A tree never has to think about whether it should grow or in which direction. It needs light, so it grows toward the sun. Even when crowded in a dense forest, a tree reaches for openings in the canopy of leaves where it can eventually soak up the rays. And a tree never wonders how high it can grow. The sky's the limit, so it keeps lifting its branches in constant, steady progress toward the sun. A tree grows continuously, providing shade and shelter while it claims its own beautiful place on the planet.

How does this compare to your personal commitment to lifelong growth? You should be constantly growing. The sky's your limit, too! Aim high, take your special place in the world. It's well worth the effort.

Enemies of Growth

The five enemies of personal growth are things you can't afford to be doing and attitudes you shouldn't have. These will stunt your growth and keep you from reaching your potential.

They are:

Public Enemy #1: Perceived lack of time

None of us has that much free time. But if you want to grow and ultimately succeed in your career, you must find some. Don't just wait for things to happen. Get off your seat and take charge of your life. Everyone has the same 24 hours in a day — what do you have to do differently to find or make the time? Even five minutes a day is better than nothing.

Public Enemy #2: Endless, repetitive tasks

It's so easy to fall under the spell of endless, repetitive tasks that steal your days away. You can do these things with one hand tied behind your back, but watch out — that's exactly what makes them an enemy to growth. These tasks are sometimes known as "busy work" because they occupy your time, even though they are meaningless and futile. Do these jobs today, and you will have to do them again tomorrow, and the next day, and the next. You won't have time to grow. You won't be able to do the more significant work that will actually help you reach your potential.

The real danger here is that you use these daily tasks as an excuse not to grow. Petty chores are the favorite tools of procrastinators. These easy and time-consuming jobs enable you to put off doing something bigger and harder that takes longer to accomplish. Yes, the important work *is* harder and will stretch you. But the alternative is remaining stagnant. You can waste your time on a treadmill of useless activities, or you can use it to accomplish something much more worthwhile.

Keep a record of how long you spend doing repetitive jobs. Eliminate the petty stuff. Fill your time with activities that bring you closer to your goals.

Public Enemy #3: Becoming a creature of habit

If you are a creature of habit, you may have a hard time with change — an attitude that can hinder your growth. A creature of habit is like an ostrich with its head in the sand. If you ignore the changes long enough, you think eventually they might go away. The other type of creature of habit is like the "cowardly lion" from *The Wizard of Oz*. When you see changes coming, you run the other way.

Whether your first impulse is to hide or bolt, neither approach works if you plan to accomplish anything in the corporate world or your professional life.

Change is not a threat. It is an opportunity to grow! And it's coming, whether you like it or not. Your employer won't stop when he or she sees the "Change is Not Welcome" sign on your door. He or she won't twist your arm in an attempt to have you embrace change. Your employer will simply find someone else who is willing and able to adjust.

Never Stop Growing

A creature of habit thinks the old way of doing things may not have been the best way, but at least it was familiar. This poor creature worries, "What if I won't be able to thrive, much less adapt, because of the change? What if I get squeezed out of the picture altogether?"

This is a misguided view. If that's your attitude, you've already identified an area of your life in which you can pursue growth. Approach the change as a challenge. Do not have a resentful attitude or dig your heels in. Cooperate, learn and think positively. Be determined and keep your expectations high. When you discover that you did adapt, the change was good, it solved a problem or made things easier, you will also discover that you not only survived, but grew! So the next time you see change coming, you won't bolt, and will know it's safe to look.

Public Enemy #4: Complacency

Complacency is an enemy of growth that can be tough to shake because it's so comfortable. Complacency means being content and self-satisfied. In relation to your career, it's a false and very smug notion that you are firmly ensconced and everything is stable and predictable.

Author James Baldwin was no fan of complacency. He said, "Even if you are on the right track, you'll get run over if you just sit there."

Complacency may seem nice, but it is like the calm before the storm. The calmness can quickly be blown away by circumstances beyond your control arriving like gale force winds, damaging your career if you're not ready.

Don't be lulled into complacency. There is nothing certain about the status quo. Make growth an ongoing activity and you will not only be moving closer to your goals, but you will be ready for whatever happens next.

Public Enemy #5: Living in the past

Nostalgia is pleasant. Looking back is fine. Learning from the past is necessary. But don't live there. If you dwell on your personal history, you won't see the potential of your future.

The past is a refuge for people who want to avoid growth. Living in the past means you don't need to worry about goals. It means thinking about what you "coulda" done, if only you could do it all over again. Or, it's believing you've done enough learning and growing and you don't need to do *that* anymore.

I suggest you leap right over this barrier to growth. Learning and growing is a lifelong process. If you stay in the past, you're giving up on your future.

Growth is a Two-Lane Highway

In order to remain marketable and make progress toward your goals, there are two ways in which you should grow.

The Close-Up View

The first kind of growth involves the knowledge and skills required to do your job. It means growth in terms of your skill set, your technical capabilities as well as your speaking, writing, listening, and computer skills.

How much longer before the knowledge and skills you have today will be outdated? With every technological advance, the bar is raised and expectations are higher. For you to remain competitive, you must be aware of the changes and constantly update and develop your skill set.

Developing your specific abilities should be a focused and strategic effort. The following exercise will help you identify the gaps between what you currently know, and what you should be learning.

1. Consider what you already know about performing *your present job*. Write down one area in which you can improve by obtaining knowledge or learning a new skill:

_____

_____

Write down the ways you can get that information.

_____

_____

2. Think about what knowledge/skills you need to get *your next job*. Identify one way you can start improving to be ready for that opportunity:

_____

_____

Where can you learn this?

_____

_____

3. Finally, think about how much longer your present skills will be up-to-date. Write down one area in which you can be proactive in developing *updated technological skills*:

_____

_____

Where can you develop these skills?

_____

_____

4. What are your barriers? How can you overcome them?

_____

_____

5. Write down your action plan.

_____

_____

The Bigger Picture

It's important to learn your job, but it's equally important to see beyond it.

Know how your role impacts your department, your company, and its bottom line. Know your company's competition and what they are doing. Don't get so caught up in your job that you lack awareness of the world beyond your desk. You can't see the bigger picture when you're looking through a magnifying glass. Educate yourself about your company, its competition, your industry, as well as technology and current events.

"I know what's going on in the world and other industries and I see how it affects my business," said Shepard. "I follow marketing trends."

Think strategically and learn what impacts your business. This knowledge, combined with your skill set, enables you to grow. And as you grow, your "market value" as an employee grows.

Growth also relates to your personal life — which has an impact on your career. Heidi M. Hunter, Vice President and Global Business Manager, Oncology at Wyeth, feels strongly about this. She said, "You need to have a life, and not only professionally. Serendipity plays a role in your career. And if you don't have a life, you're going to miss out. You should do new things all the time so you'll continually grow."

Exercise:

1. What suggestions can you think of that may help your firm save money or improve its bottom line? This can be operations-related, for example: different daily systems.

_____

_____

_____

2. What trends exist in your industry that your firm can learn from and/or capitalize on?

_____

_____

_____

3. Think about your competitors and compare marketing materials, Web sites, and other information you learn about them. Write down three things that they're doing better than your firm. Then, list any measures you can take or suggest to eliminate this advantage and ensure your company is superior in this area.

_____

_____

_____

Your Growth Action Plan

Reaching your potential requires an ongoing commitment to growth. I've discussed how developing your abilities makes you more marketable, keeps you from becoming a dinosaur, and brings you closer to your goals.

Continuing Your Formal Education

The most rewarding and highly regarded effort you can make is obtaining a degree that will help you progress in your career. Do you need to complete your bachelor's degree? Would an MBA or other graduate-level degree be an asset? If you've already obtained these degrees, why not work toward a Ph.D.? If you think a doctorate is something only other people get — remember my advice in chapter one. Be proactive. Find your own opportunities.

"You need to constantly challenge yourself," said Jo Anne Rolle Harper, Vice President, Sales Steere Pharmaceuticals, for Pfizer. "I have taken MBA-level classes and participated in in-house training."

Furthering your education *is* possible. You can even pursue your education online, taking courses wherever your computer takes you!

Complete one or two courses a semester, and in a few years you will have your degree. You can't slow the passage of time, but you *can* choose when you will do it. When you're looking back two years from now, your hands could be empty, or they could be holding your new diploma.

It's not a matter of whether you have the ability or time to continue your education; it's whether you *choose* to do it.

Certifications and Licenses

In addition to advanced degrees, you need to have the professional certifications and licenses that prove you are an expert and committed to your career. If you are in finance, for example, get certified as a financial advisor. Be a CPA, not just an accountant. These certifications give you instant credibility as far as your working knowledge and capabilities are concerned.

Pursue certifications and obtain licenses that enable you to become more specialized, or to branch out in new career directions.

Sheryl Craun, Vice President of Client Services for ADP Retirement Services, has been committed to pursuing knowledge throughout her career. She has professional certifications and licenses directly related to her job, plus others, which are more diversified. Craun has accumulated a plethora of credentials, including Myers-Briggs and ERISSA certifications and licenses. She is currently pursuing a master's degree in financial planning. Craun advises women to keep growing. "Learn your job and then look for what's next," she said.

Once you've got those credentials, don't neglect them. Dr. Catherine E. Palmier, Chief Medical Officer, United Healthcare of Georgia, stresses the importance of pursuing your education and keeping your certifications up-to-date. "Go to school," she said. "Keep up with your certifications. Never let a part of what you've done go by the wayside."

In-House Training or Other Workshops

If your company offers training seminars or similar workshops, you should also pursue knowledge by attending. Go to your training department and sign up for classes that will enhance your "market value."

If your firm doesn't already offer such options, tell your HR director or supervisor that you are interested in attending such a program. Perhaps if they hear this feedback, and others in your department agree, your company *will* start offering training or coaching. If not, find places where you can take programs — at local colleges, association conferences, on the Internet, etc.

Diana Ruddick, Vice President, Distribution Development & Communications at MassMutual Financial Group, takes courses through the firm. Her goal is to complete 40 hours of continuing education courses every year. She also reads 10 to 12 business books in any given year, which she finds useful as a knowledge source.

Reading

You'll gain a world of knowledge by reading. Reading can motivate, inspire and teach you. It enables you to keep abreast of changes in the world and technology. It helps you learn about your company as well as its competition.

This knowledge makes you a more valuable employee. It also enables you to have intelligent discussions with colleagues and clients, and make informed small talk at networking events.

Read avidly as you pursue growth. The women I interviewed read for business, inspiration and fun. Each woman has her favorite sources, and individual choices include management books, leadership articles, industry publications, *The Wall Street Journal*, *Harvard Business Review*, *Forbes*, the Bible, fiction, Web sites, and online articles.

Debra Brown-Spruill, Executive Director of OCLC — Public Affairs Information Services, reads at least one newspaper a day, as well as magazines and Internet news groups. She said, "What you know at 25 won't define you at 35. It's only a beginning, not the end of anything."

Share and circulate publications with other employees. It's an excellent way to "break the ice" and develop your professional relationships.

Look for books on tape and CD, and listen to them on the ride to work, during business travel, and when you exercise.

Be Mentored

Another way to grow is to find a mentor. The women I interviewed for this book — all highly successful in their chosen fields — felt that having mentors was imperative. Some also believe that many women tend to have problems getting mentors unlike their male colleagues.

What is mentoring? Mentoring is an opportunity to learn and grow, a chance to share what you've experienced and what you want to understand. It is also a chance to hear new perspectives on the business and industry in which you are involved.

There are many groups in a variety of industries that foster and promote mentoring relationships. One such entity is the Healthcare Businesswomen's Association (HBA). Dr. Catherine A. Sohn, Vice President Worldwide Business Development, Consumer Healthcare, at GlaxoSmithKline, has been involved in mentoring programs in HBA for years. She said this has helped her grow professionally, contributing to her overall success.

There are benefits gained by the mentor and mentee throughout the mentoring relationship. Cheryl Doll, Vice President of Marketing at LodgeWorks, said, "I've had mentors who were inclusive. They would take me to meetings where I couldn't contribute, but learned more by watching — and it positioned me well." She now tries this with her own direct reports. "Being there helped me get here," Doll said. Another mentor taught her, "It takes a servant heart to lead." Doll explained, "The idea is that by promoting others, you promote yourself."

Mentoring is not usually about a specific task or role. Mentoring tends to be broader, encompassing larger life and business goals. For example, a person may seek a mentor who has been a successful business owner because he or she has an interest in developing his or her own business, or a young executive may seek out a more experienced executive to assist in "learning the ropes" at a company.

People look for mentors from whom they can learn a number of things about their type of work, industry, success secrets, how they balance multiple demands, and their way of thinking and approaching varied situations. Mentoring relationships occur because the mentor has some kind of "work/life expertise," not primarily because he or she has "skill expertise."

In Peggie Pelosi-Gardiner's case, her mentors were not all in the multi-level marketing industry. Pelosi-Gardiner, the Vice President of Network Development for USANA Health Sciences, said her initial mentors were family friends and people she met through personal development programs.

Beverly Holmes, Senior Vice President, Executive Officer, Retirement Services, at Mass Mutual Financial Group, mentors many people. She encourages them to make changes where appropriate sometimes with their communication style, their dress, their hair, and the way they interact with decision makers. "Your demeanor can leave the perception that you are not strong or focused, or can take on a challenge," she said.

Mentors do not necessarily have to be well-versed in the mentee's line of work or even the specific position held. The discussions and interactions focus on opportunities and challenges that the mentee is experiencing and how to navigate through them.

Finally, like creating advocates, mentoring is all about the relationship. Mentors and mentees tend to discuss aspects of one's personal and business lives, therefore there has to be a certain level of trust, respect and friendship for this to happen effectively.

Think of mentors as people who have already "been there, done that" — and, more importantly, are willing to share what happened along the way.

Brown-Spruill has had many mentors. One, she explained, was a woman who hired her, and said, "I want you to learn from the mistakes I made. Don't just quit. Try to make it work in this environment. Learn the politics within the organization."

Mentoring and/or being mentored is a great way to aid in your personal and professional development — the attainment of which, needs to be a never-ending "homework" assignment.

Get a Coach

Like mentoring, being coached can help you grow as a professional. Unlike a mentor, however, a professional coach uses a combination of assessment tools and instruments to help you better identify yourself and your behavioral traits.

Wouldn't it be nice if everyone was born with "boardroom presence?" The reality is that many women get passed over when it comes to promotions and partnerships because they lack the expected social graces, political savvy and communication skills. These professionals can seek out executive coaching so that they can get the help needed.

Exactly what is an executive coach? The idea is the same as a sports coach — where a coach works on the player's specific issues or problems. The sports coach listens, observes the player's game and attitudes, and strives to eliminate ineffective behaviors.

A coach meets face to face with you, or on the phone, and tries to get inside your head — what's working well and what thought processes need to be improved. An effective coach strives to eliminate any negative influences in your life — personal and at work — that may be preventing you from achieving your goals.

By their very nature, coaches are objective "outsiders" who can look in and see the "full picture." They help their professional clients list objectives, and find effective systems to use to implement desired changes.

When I am hired for coaching initiatives to coach individuals on their professionalism and presence, I first interview their peers, subordinates, and managers regarding all aspects of communication. Armed with this input, along with my own observations, I then give each "player" very specific feedback. They then develop an action plan for change. Over time, depending on their needs, I will videotape them, attend networking events or meetings to "shadow" them, even take them shopping. There are weekly assignments, plus telephone coaching to help them through various situations. I also touch base with their managers and ask for feedback regarding observable change. Periodically, I also involve the client's spouse or significant other to help on the home front.

The success rate has been excellent. To date, everyone I have coached to become a vice president or partner has become one. In some situations, I also have designed interventions which combine individual coaching and group training.

Coaching is a molding, refining strategy and cuts right to the core of the issues. It helps employees solve problems and find their own new ways to succeed and grow.

How does the company benefit? Once people, the most important asset, feel secure, confident, dedicated and successful, company profit improves. Everybody wins with coaching.

Growth is Your Responsibility

Don't wait for others to present you with growth opportunities. You have to take the first step, and every step, in your action plan. You have to let others know what you want to do. And, if necessary, you have to pay for it!

You may find that your company is a good financial resource for pursuing your education. Your employer may be generous enough to pay for subscriptions to worthwhile publications, membership in trade associations, attendance at training seminars and conferences, and even reimburse your tuition if you choose to pursue a degree. After all, your professional development is a smart corporate investment. If your company does not support your efforts financially, however, remember that growth is, ultimately, *your* responsibility. Your company's lack of financial support should not deter you from pursuing opportunities.

Don't be afraid to invest in yourself financially. Your investment is likely to pay for itself when your growth leads to a better job, promotion, and self-improvement.

Effective growth involves risk. There's no way around this fact. That being said, however, this shouldn't deter you from digging in and improving your professional "roots."

Kim Woodworth, Divisional Vice President, Comcast Advertising Sales, for Comcast Corp., is not afraid to take risks. She has switched industries and started new offices. Woodworth said she's learned by change and is not fearful. "The more you step out of your comfort zone, the more you learn."

Risk-Taking Results in Growth

I believe that the people who grow the most are the ones who are willing to takes risks. You can't grow if you are not willing to move beyond what's familiar and safe. Growth can't happen if you think it's better to leave well enough alone. If circumstances in your career seem stable and predictable now, the reality is, they are not.

Your circumstances could change dramatically, unpredictably, overnight, in ways that you couldn't foresee, control or even fathom. Avoiding risk is not a guarantee for security.

In fact, taking risks may actually be the attitude that enables you to protect your career and your future through the shifting fortunes of the business world. People want to be safe and secure. But nothing is safe and secure. Taking a risk could enable you to step off the rug before it gets pulled out from under your feet. As hard as risk taking can be, you might as well take the plunge.

When considering whether or not to take a risk, think about what's stopping you. If it's one of the enemies of growth discussed earlier in this chapter, especially complacency and a penchant for living in the past, it is not a good reason.

The risks worth taking are strategic and calculated in nature. Make sure you are not simply pursuing a "castle in the sky." If the benefits are great enough, it's worth the risk. If it's a high risk with the potential of high reward, you could surprise yourself with a spectacular outcome. If it's a high risk with low reward, forget it. Find a better opportunity.

Whether it's accepting a challenging promotion or a lateral move, volunteering for a task force or new position, or even relocating, the decisions that push you forward in your career usually involve an element of risk.

When asked to list an important activity she has participated in, or an action taken during her career in order to achieve success, Lisa Reeves, Senior Vice President of SAP Ventures, said, "Doing projects that no one else wanted — those that are time consuming, messy, challenging or those that needed consensus. These were turning points for me. If you succeed at these projects, it gets you success and visibility working with senior people."

The rewarding and satisfying position that I'm in right now is due to the fact that I created a completely new challenge for myself after being a professor for 22 years. I was a tenured professor, secure in my job. I also had the responsibility of being a single mom with two teenage girls. But I needed a change and wanted to grow. I had a vision of starting my own training and consulting business, but I didn't have any business background. I decided to discuss the idea with my dad.

"Are you crazy?" he said. He reminded me strongly that I had two children to support and I should be mindful of my responsibilities.

I then talked to Alan, the man I was dating, now my husband. He asked me two questions that I still refer to today when considering risks:

What's the worst that can happen? This is the first question you must ask yourself. Consider the worst possible outcome of taking the risk. In my case, the worst case scenario was that I would fail, with no way to support myself or my children.

Then what? Will you land on your feet if you fail? As long as you have a good backup plan, consider taking a risk that may propel you to grow and have a more successful career. I realized that taking the risk to quit my teaching job wasn't going to leave me without resources to fall back on. I could always get another teaching position, or I could take a corporate sales or training job. The risk no longer seemed so frightening.

Besides, failing at something doesn't make you a failure. You will always learn something.

Best of all, I was bolstered by the faith that my daughters had in me. They both assured me of their trust. They said they knew that I would always be able to care for their needs.

As you evaluate your decision to take a risk and seek the advice of others, know that you will encounter people who discourage you. They may do this for various reasons. Some of these naysayers are negative just for the sake of being negative, or they are protecting themselves, or fearful for you. I think a lot of the discouragement comes from people who look back at their own lives regretfully because of risks they didn't take.

Many of the successful women I interviewed have been empowered and successful due to their willingness to take calculated risks. They recall that the pivotal moments in their careers occurred when significant risk was involved.

"I left my job after 15 years when I could have stayed forever," said Catherine J. Ross, President, Security Services for Day & Zimmermann. She left to become president of a competitor company in the same industry. The only thing Ross would have done differently with 20-20 hindsight, is research the industry she entered more thoroughly. "In retrospect, I'd have at least explored my options and then made decisions. I was always happy where I was and had never accepted the invitations from executive search firms, or competitors in the industry, to discuss other opportunities." Still, Ross is glad she took the risk, as there are more opportunities for her growth.

A successful female executive from the financial services industry said she resigned as an employment lawyer and started a new job in human resources at age 51. "Talented people always land on their feet," she said.

Risks can mean navigating your way through uncharted territories.

Sheryl Craun, Vice President of Client Services for ADP Retirement Services, said she took risks that involved relocating as well as starting new divisions and departments within her firm. "I was willing to move out of state several times. I'd leave a job without having a job," she said.

With a compass pointing to the future, use your intelligence and experience to find your way. Be flexible,

---

Checklist for Enhancing Your Skillset & Knowledge

Things you can do:

- Take a class at a local college or university, online, or via the regular mail, to pursue your degree.
- Get requisite certifications and licenses.
- Become familiar with all content in your company's annual report and Web site.
- Read business-related books to enhance your knowledge base.
- Subscribe to magazines and journals in your industry, or specific to your role. If your responsibilities are training in nature, you should be reading *T+D* and *Training* magazines. If you are in sales, you should be reading *Selling Power* and *Selling*.
- Read business newspapers, like *The Wall Street Journal*, *Investor's Business Daily* and *Financial Times*.
- Surf the Internet and read all industry-relevant Web pages and articles.
- Participate in trade associations which offer certifications, publications, regular meetings, training, and opportunities for you to lead, speak and write.
- Take training courses.
- Get a coach.
- Be mentored.

---

have faith. Know that even if you make mistakes, you have tried your best. You have grown.

Risk-Taking Exercise:

What is one risk you would be willing to take in business?

_____

_____

What's the worst that could happen if you take that risk?

_____

_____

Then what? What would you be able to do if you fail?

_____

_____

Once you consider the potential outcomes, including the possible rewards and solutions if you fail, the risk may not be so frightening. Consider taking a risk that could move you further toward your potential. Make sure you are well positioned, and make taking the risk one part of your overall growth plan.

"Don't ever stop working on yourself and who you want to become," said the successful woman from the financial services industry.

Remember, if you aren't green and growing, you are ripe and rotting. What are you committed to do to grow?

Chapter 5 ~ I
Increase Your Involvement

You've come a long way on the road to reaching your potential — perhaps even further than you realize! That's because, by improving your **Manner**, developing **Advocates** and finding ways to **Grow**, you've already begun the next process in your own marketing plan: Involvement, the "I" in **MAGIC.**

Do you see now how it's all coming together? Far from being independent, all the parts of my **MAGIC** formula work together, and will impact each other and your overall efforts. Yes, separately, each aspect of self-marketing you've read thus far may be effective in gaining some exposure. But, COMBINE them all, and you'll be well on your way to securing plenty of ammunition to score big career successes.

Two more strategies left to explore … starting with getting more involved. It's time to shift your involvement level into high gear, with a strategic focus and plan.

You Get Great Returns on <u>This</u> Investment

Involvement is an investment with guaranteed rewards. When you get involved strategically in organizations and activities, you will not only be helping your company, your colleagues or a worthy cause, you will also be helping your career. Involvement leads to more success.

"The advantage of being involved is you meet people, learn interesting things, and you give back," said Aida Levitan, Ph.D., CEO of Publicis Sanchez & Levitan.

Jo Anne Rolle Harper, Vice President, Sales for the Steere Pharmaceuticals division of Pfizer Inc., also attests to the benefits of being involved. She has been a volunteer for Luminaires, Orange County, CA, that raised money and supported the Doheney Eye Institute. Rolle Harper also volunteered as a Board Member for the Juvenile Diabetes Research Foundation in Fairfield, CT. Now she is focusing on getting involved in internal activities at Pfizer. "Involvement enables me to meet interesting people. It has given me resources which are essential for being in senior management," she said.

Involvement starts with a willingness to serve. It requires you to contribute your time and talents for the benefit of others, but it pays you back with countless opportunities in which you can grow, meet people and gain positive visibility.

"I chose external involvement as a mechanism for growth," said Judith E. Tschirgi, Chief Information Officer & Senior Vice President, SEI Investments. "For example, I wanted to learn about boards, so I joined a nonprofit board to learn."

Growth Factor

Take an active role in areas beyond your job responsibilities and you will grow both personally and professionally. You will gain recognition and learn skills needed to advance your career. Seek out roles that stretch you, that require you to develop your leadership, negotiation and communication skills. You will look back on your accomplishments with pride, and feel more confident of your abilities in the future.

"Involvement in the nonprofit sector allowed me to develop as a leader," said Peggi Einhorn, Senior Vice President, JPMorganChase, of her role as past Chairperson of the board for the Brooklyn Children's Museum. "I became a public spokesperson, set strategic direction for the institution, galvanized leadership from fellow trustees and ran countless board and executive committee meetings," she said. These experiences carried over to her banking career. "Taking a higher profile at work came more naturally ... and people's expectations of me changed as I demonstrated success 'as a leader' in a different sphere."

"For me, external involvement drove the internal rise," said Christine L. James-Brown, President & CEO of United Way of Southeastern Pennsylvania. "It wouldn't have happened without the outside. My advice is to get involved in outside organizations, get on boards. My volunteer work was great for me personally and for the United Way."

People Magnet

If you want to expand your network, develop advocates and gain visibility, you must become actively involved in your company, industry and community. Your activities add to your value, and show people what you are capable of doing.

"Through my volunteer work, people see how hardworking I am," said Ada C. Nielsen, Manager, Commercial Development, Nitriles Licensing, for BP Chemicals. "Getting involved in associations and outside activities enabled me to meet people who gave me referrals, which is how I got all my jobs."

Stop Making Excuses; Start Getting Involved

Dr. Betty L. Siegel, President of Kennesaw State University, said it best: "Get really involved with any group you can."

There's no good excuse for avoiding involvement and leadership roles. Don't let feelings of apprehension and insecurity hold you back. I know from personal experience that when you put doubt aside and get actively involved, rewards and recognition will follow.

I was the classic non-joiner. Working hard, raising a family, my thought was that I just didn't have time to get involved. I was reluctant to extend myself any further or take on more commitments. It took a lot of convincing before I finally joined the Mid-Atlantic Chapter of the National Speakers Association.

For two years, I kept my involvement level low. I attended meetings, enjoying opportunities to listen to interesting speakers and learn from the experiences they shared. I met nice people. Then, I was asked if I would sit at the registration desk for future meetings. My role would be to meet and greet members as they arrived, and collect attendance fees. I agreed, and found it was an excellent way to get to know everyone in the group. A year later, when I was asked to serve on the program committee, I agreed. The following year, I served as chairperson of the program committee. Then, I was asked to be on the chapter's board. Shortly after I agreed to this, I was asked if I would accept the role of president-elect, which would ultimately lead to becoming president. My involvement level was like a snowball getting bigger as it rolled down a mountain, and now I was afraid there was an avalanche headed my way! I got scared.

Me, president of the association? This could involve a lot more time than I thought I had. I also doubted my leadership skills, so I assumed I would have my work cut out for me. Would this role be worth the time and effort I needed to invest? I decided to get some informed opinions. I asked the presidents of five other trade associations about their experiences. Was it worthwhile? Each person gave me the same answer: "I got much more than I gave."

What did they gain from this high level of involvement? Confidence, leadership abilities, negotiation skills and exposure. Yes, it was definitely worth it.

I took the position, and I must say it was a great relief when my year of duty was over. It was a commitment that involved a lot of time and effort, but it is a year I am proud of. People saw that I am reliable and a hard worker, and they viewed me in a way they never did before — as a leader and negotiator. In addition to having the title of "past president," and an advisor, I now have greater confidence in my abilities and valuable new career skills. Not to mention I got connected nationally within the association, which led to referrals and new friends.

The experience also helped me understand the advantages of strategically seeking involvement and leadership roles. Becoming president of the Mid-Atlantic Chapter of the National Speakers Association was not on my original list of goals. Why not? Because back then, I was staying behind self-imposed barriers to involvement which I thought were protecting my time and what I perceived as my lack of ability. When I overcame those barriers and took the risk (remember, taking risks is part of growth!), I got involved and made a breakthrough that gave me exposure and enhanced my career.

What's Stopping You?

There are three excuses people typically give for not getting actively involved in areas beyond their immediate job responsibilities:

1. "I never thought about it before."

People often compartmentalize their lives, separating work roles and home life to the extent that there is very little, if any, overlap. To a certain point, this is good, because we all need time to unwind and get out of the spotlight by relaxing in our personal lives. But it's not good if that mentality causes us to overlook people and opportunities. Networks and advocacy can develop practically anywhere. Your next advocate could be someone on your professional association *or* someone you meet at your child's soccer game. Think strategically and make time for growth any time you see the opportunity.

Gail Evans, former Executive Vice President, CNN News Group, thinks that, as a boss, it's important to demonstrate balance in her life. She is involved with her children's activities and volunteers to work on committees. "Women often think that organizations in your personal life, like charities and your kids' schools, are only personal. I don't agree," she said. "You will meet people who have connections to people in business. Get to know moms who are home raising their kids. They can talk to their husbands and this can affect your career."

Evans is author of the popular books *She Wins, You Win* and *Play Like A Man Win Like A Woman.*

A successful executive from the consumer goods industry agreed. "Now I'm involved with my children's school and sports organizations and I've gotten to know people who can help me in future career-related pursuits," she said.

2.   "I don't feel confident enough ... I don't have the skills."

If you lack confidence or think that you are limited in certain skills, then involvement is *exactly* what you need.

Involvement isn't an ordeal; it's an opportunity. Don't avoid involvement; seek it out! Involvement gives you confidence as it helps develop your leadership skills. It provides opportunities to learn, and resources when you need help.

You won't be alone in pursuing involvement as a way to build confidence and abilities. Most of the other professionals in the group or activity will be doing the same thing!

Irene Horstmann Hannan, Senior Vice President & Director, Women's Business Services, at Wachovia, spent many years volunteering for not-for-profit organizations and continues to serve on boards. She chaired the Cross-roads School, which was a challenging role, but one in which she had a valuable opportunity to grow. "It was a real test of my ability to cut it," she said. "It gave me a shot of confidence and a new skill set. I've integrated these skills with my career goals."

3.   "I don't have time."

We all have the same 24 hours a day. Perhaps you could be more efficient with how you use your time.

Begin by cutting out unproductive activities that are time robbers at work and home, and do things that lead to the more important goal of reaching your potential. Manage your personal time more efficiently. Do fewer errands, less housework. Your house won't fall down under the weight of a little extra dust! At your job, do less of the busy work I warned you about in the previous chapter. Be strategic about where you choose to get involved. Don't spread yourself too thin. Pick one area of involvement that will have the biggest impact for you.

"Time is gold," said Levitan. "When you are involved, be selective. Be involved in a big way, don't just put your name out there."

Talk to your manager about all the places where you are involved, the requirements of having an active role, and the rewards in terms of how it will make you a better employee or help your company. Your manager may encourage your efforts and agree to let you perform some of your related duties on company time. Your employer may also see the value of having workers represent the company through involvement in charitable and community endeavors, and will encourage and recognize you for this. If not, it's still your responsibility to make the time and be strategic about what you do.

"You will need to be very creative if you are part of a company which discourages outside professional relationships due to concerns about competition," said Dr. Catherine E. Palmier of United Healthcare of Georgia, where she is Chief Medical Officer. "In those cases," she explained, "your past, professional acquaintances will be critical to your network. You may need to seek those out through strictly social channels, in order to maintain your professional relationships, and also satisfy your employer's guidelines."

Palmier added, "I learned this the hard way with a former employer — I found myself seeking new opportunities with a very limited professional network, because I neglected to maintain key relationships."

Where to Get Involved

Perhaps you've heard the quote by Sidney Lanier, "If you want to be found, stand where the seekers seek" — it nicely summarizes my point about how to get more involved.

This statement means that you should position yourself strategically to gain exposure that will help achieve your career goals. Where will you find decision makers and potential advocates? Ask people in your company, your field, and the community. Talk to them about what they do to get involved.

Determine where the right people are, and then make sure you are in the same place.

A friend of mine, Peter, recently made a strategic decision regarding involvement. Peter works in the finance department of a *Fortune* 500 company. His goal is to become CFO of a mid-sized corporation. He decided to join a very expensive country club. He and his wife agreed it was a worthwhile expense, and, therefore, would give up other things in order to afford membership.

I asked why he wanted to join the club. He explained that people in finance are expected to play golf, and he needed to lower his handicap. Peter also wanted to get on the club's board of directors. I asked why he felt he had to belong to this particular club, since it was quite expensive. He said, "Where do you think the people who will hire me belong?" Belonging to the expensive club was part of Peter's strategic plan for advancing his career, and, therefore, a smart investment. Peter was positioning himself to meet influential people and gain exposure with the ultimate goal of getting what he wants in his career.

My friend Mary is an example of how involvement pays off. Mary had her own public relations firm, but after moving to a new city, she had to start the business all over again. She came up with a game plan to get new clients and generate the business she needed to be successful. Mary got involved with the local Rotary Club and symphony orchestra. Then, she got on the boards of these organizations. Within a few years, thanks to the visibility Mary created in these roles and the people she

131

met, her public relations business was flourishing. She established herself strategically by taking active roles in significant organizations. It was just what her career needed.

Hopefully, you are beginning to think about opportunities for involvement that will benefit your career. There are three areas you should consider: within your company, in a professional association, and in community and charitable organizations. When choosing an area of involvement, think strategically about the possibilities and opportunities that exist in each situation. Think about what skills you need to develop and where you can obtain them. It's also important to consider what areas of involvement may give you the most value to your employer, but don't be limited.

1.   Within Your Company

Participate internally beyond your job responsibilities. You can contribute within your company by serving on task forces and teams. Volunteer for projects and committees in which you have a valuable role and can make strategic connections. Go for maximum visibility.

Get involved with company activities. Assist company-supported charities like the United Way. Help plan company events.

Join the company golf team. In days past, men ruled the golf course when it came to networking and deal making. But today, women are successfully crossing into the let's-do-business-on-the-golf-course world, taking advantage of an activity that is enjoyable and good for their careers. Work on your game and use it to develop relationships and build your business successes.

Lisa Reeves, Senior Vice President of SAP Ventures, is very involved within the firm and is a member of many teams. As a result, she said, "I am seen as someone who is willing to take on projects by senior management and the board. I'm seen as a leader who executes."

2. Professional Associations

When considering areas of involvement in your field of expertise, look at the bigger picture — the professional arena outside your company. This includes women's and business organizations, trade or industry associations.

If you are a business owner, you need to join your local Chamber of Commerce. Also consider joining at least one other association for business owners. Your membership could enable you to participate in group health insurance and take advantage of special business loan programs.

Consider becoming a member of the National Association of Women Business Owners (NAWBO) or the National Association for Female Executives (NAFE). These organizations also have local chapters that meet regularly and enable you to connect with other professional women.

You will benefit greatly from your involvement in professional associations. These groups provide members with education seminars that often meet qualifications for continuing education credits. Many associations also award industry designations to members who meet qualifications. For example, I earned my CSP (Certified Speaking Professional) designation from the National Speakers Association, and the title Certified Management Consultant (CMC) from the Institute of Management Consultants.

Associations also may offer technical assistance, scholarship opportunities and awards. There may be annual conferences at a national level that can help with sales and adding new clients.

Through these organizations, you can build your network, share ideas, and develop relationships with people you can call when advice or technical assistance is needed.

"I tell everyone they should find, join and become active in trade associations," said Debra Brown-Spruill, Executive Director, OCLC — Public Affairs Information Services. "Meet people outside your company. You will need it someday because it develops relationships. Join associations. They are critical for success."

Talk to people and find out what associations they belong to. Do a Web search of associations in your industry. Visit the Web sites and find out which associations have local chapters and where they meet. Then, choose a group, become a member, and start attending!

3. Community and Charitable Organizations

Don't underestimate the power of getting involved in community and charitable organizations. These groups are eager for volunteers. Your involvement is a way to help others while meeting people and developing skills that transfer to your career.

Many executives that I interviewed for this book contribute their time and efforts to worthy causes such as the Rotary, Lions Clubs, American Red Cross, American Diabetes Association and Habitat for Humanity. Choose an organization that matters to you, roll up your sleeves, and get to work. And don't be surprised if you're working right next to a person who can help your career.

Volunteer in ways that help children — yours or others. Contribute your time and efforts to Boy Scouts or Girl Scouts of America, Big Brothers/Big Sisters of America, or Little League. Volunteer to coach the soccer or baseball team.

"When my kids were younger, I was involved in PTA," said Sue Rusch. "It helped my visibility and I learned leadership skills."

These are great opportunities to bond with your children (if you have them) and help others in your community (even if you have no children of your own). They are also great ways for you to expand your network of people who can ultimately help you. And, just think about what you may learn in the process!

Get involved within your church or synagogue, and attend services. You may find you are enhancing your spiritual *and* professional life. A house of worship is common ground, drawing people together from all walks of life. It is also a place where you may develop an advocate or mentor.

Get to know the people in your community, condo association, or gym, and then find ways to get involved so you are seen as a leader.

Take the Initiative, Be Active

Why not create your own opportunities for involvement?

Within your company or industry, what are the needs? Take the initiative and start a committee or task force to address those needs. You will get great exposure and others will view you as a motivated and hardworking person who is ready to take on a challenge.

The goal with involvement is tiered — first, learn more about the group, its mission and any opportunities available. Then, get to know the people and make sure they get to know you. This is a low level of involvement, and it is appropriate in the beginning. Then you must take the next step and become actively involved.

Active involvement requires you to do more than merely attend meetings and mingle with others. Take an active role by speaking up, contributing, and volunteering when you see a need. Volunteer for small roles first. Ultimately, become a leader.

Within professional associations, first volunteer to be on committees. Then, seek to become a director or officer on the board. If asked to serve in these roles, say yes! Within your company, volunteer to serve on a team, task force or committee. Then, volunteer to be the leader.

Toot Your Horn

Let all advocates and managers know about your outside (and internal) involvements and any leadership roles. These people are in a position to help you advance in your career. Keep them informed of your increasing value!

"I gain visibility and recognition for my accomplishments by working hard and participating in groups," said a female executive from the investment industry, "I let others know that I teach at NYU. I let others know that I'm a volunteer for Boys and Girls Clubs of America. I toot my own horn. No one else will do it for you."

Keep a file or set up a database that lists what you've done and the roles you have had. Refer to it when it's time for a review, you're up for a promotion, or when updating your resume.

Leadership: The Ultimate Investment of Involvement

Don't just get involved and be a follower. Seek opportunities to grow as a leader.

Suzanne Fairlie, President of Pro Search, Inc., said, "Leaders in the workplace, as in life, are those who have learned how to lead the dance, not ask to be danced."

Leadership ability is quite possibly the most important character trait you can have in the corporate world. Some people are born leaders. Others have to work at it. And like so many other factors in your personal success, becoming a leader is a choice. It's not a question of whether you *can* lead, it's whether you will choose to do so.

How do you become a leader? Some professionals are thrown unexpectedly into leadership roles and find that they had the ability to lead within themselves all along. A wise person seizes such serendipitous opportunities; but it's even wiser to strategically go after any chance to hold a leadership position. Do not wait for such an opportunity to fall into your lap. You might not be so lucky!

Tell your boss, all advocates, senior management, the leaders of your association, or anyone else in a position to help you advance, what you hope to accomplish through your involvements. After all, you can't expect to be offered an opportunity if you don't let people know what you are willing to do.

"I made it known that I wanted to be elected to various boards that had a genuine interest in adult learning and economic development specifically focused on women," said Beverly Holmes, Senior Vice President, Executive Officer, Retirement Services at MassMutual Financial Group.

Share with others your desire to lead, and then demonstrate it. Show that you have initiative.

Cheryl Doll, Vice President of Marketing for LodgeWorks, shows people that she is a leader by taking on challenges. "I am always game to tackle a new and tough assignment," she said. "There are always a lot of executors, but few who can create."

Speak clearly about your willingness to lead. Women often have a self-defeating tendency to beat around the bush when it comes to communicating what they want. Maybe it's the internal barrier that tells women not to make waves, to just work hard and hope someone notices. Or maybe it's a concern about appearing too eager or pushy.

Most women know that success doesn't happen if they think that way. People don't have the ability to read your mind. Your manager and advocates have their own responsibilities and are not likely to spend time or energy figuring out what you might want to do with your life.

When an influential person tells you about a leadership opportunity, don't hedge about your interest. Don't make the mistake of responding in a self-effacing manner. The guy in the next cubicle who wants the same opportunity won't be so humble. He is already thinking strategically about control and power. If your words suggest that maybe you can't handle the leadership role, the person who made the offer will probably believe you.

Don't downplay your ability. A leader expresses her goals and ambitions. She has high expectations!

The 21 Indispensable Qualities of a Leader:
Becoming the Person Others Will Want to Follow
by John C. Maxwell

Character	Focus	Relationships
Charisma	Generosity	Responsibility
Commitment	Initiative	Security
Communications	Listening	Self-discipline
Competence	Passion	Servanthood
Courage	Positive attitude	Teachability
Discernment	Problem solving	Vision

Another inappropriate response when asked to lead is, "Well all right, I'll do it if you're really stuck." Accept the offer graciously or, if it would hinder rather than help your career strategy, decline it respectfully.

If you feel nervous or insecure about leading, it's even more important that you lead. Most people find that assuming a new leadership role is a daunting and possibly risky endeavor, so you are not alone. But think through my risk-taking questions in chapter four. What's the worst that could happen if you take the role? Suppose you fail as a leader. That possibility seems extremely unlikely, but just suppose you did. Then what? You would recover. Be determined that, no matter what, you will learn from every experience in your career and you will try again.

What are the qualities of a good leader? You may be surprised to learn that "the right stuff" doesn't necessarily mean things that men do best. A good leader is intuitive and compassionate. Women have those qualities naturally! A good leader is also reliable, hard working, independent and flexible. Doesn't it sound like I am describing *you*? A good leader also knows how to tap into the strengths of the people she is leading, whether it's on a board, task force, team or committee.

You don't need to be tough to be an effective leader. People don't respond well to a leader who is overbearing or aggressive, especially if that leader is a woman. A good leader brings out the best in people by showing she has faith in them. She keeps her sense of humor when facing adversity.

Leadership is a necessary part of your plan for career success. It gives you authority and credibility, in addition to experience and skills that can carry over throughout your career.

When you invest your time and effort to lead others, you will never experience a loss. You get back even more in terms of personal and professional growth.

You will grow in character, leadership ability and knowledge. You will make someone's job easier, and his or her life better. You will increase your value to employers, advocates, and others whose lives you touch. You will make and strengthen connections with people. Value those connections not only for the opportunities they afford your career, but for the richness and joy they can add to your life.

Suzanne Fairlie, President of Pro Search, Inc., said, "I like leading. I work closely with my clients, and like to give. I enjoy giving free career advice, market advice, and other free help. In the long run, it's a two-way street, but you have to initiate the giving, and not keep close tabs on the score. And, I enjoy getting back, too." She is on the Union League's business advisory board, the Junior Achievement board, the Pinnacle board, and a member of Forum of Executive Women.

Dr. Catherine A. Sohn, Vice President Worldwide Business Development, Consumer Healthcare at GlaxoSmithKline, is involved with many outside activities and boards of directors, and for four primary reasons. She said, "I get energy from other enthusiastic and positive people. I get ideas from other companies to bring back. It's fun. I like to give back and help."

"Getting involved is crucial to achieving visibility and driving success in whatever you do," said Roslyn Courtney, a leadership expert and executive coach. "That's the way you learn and learn how to contribute in new and different arenas. Seek out the opportunities, add your ideas to making the big project better ... learn from and observe role models, peers and competitive businesses. Don't be afraid to step up to the plate." Courtney is leading a major initiative to study exemplary women leaders, and develops innovative tools to help women become leaders at all stages of their careers.

The rewards of increased involvement *will* be immeasurable. The journey to your potential — which never really ends — will be a more fulfilling trip.

Involvement Opportunity Worksheet

1. Where in your company can you get involved?

_____

_____

2. In what trade or business associations can you get involved?

_____

_____

3. Other involvement opportunities:

Church or synagogue: _____

Charitable organizations: _____

Community: _____

Other: _____

_____

From your list of ideas, choose one area or organization in which you will become actively involved. Make your choice strategically.

Next steps for joining: _____

Commitment date: _____

Identify a leadership opportunity: _____

_____

Chapter 6 ～ C
Create Commentary

Step Into the Spotlight

Thomas Edison said, "If we did all the things we are capable of doing, we would literally astonish ourselves."

Well, prepare for some astonishment! By growing and getting involved, you have taken giant steps on the journey to reaching your full potential. Far from being the hardworking but invisible woman you once were, you are now thinking and acting strategically, standing up and speaking out, connecting with others, and taking control. Those giant steps have brought you to a point where you can, and should, claim your place in the spotlight.

You've reached the **C** in **MAGIC** — Create Commentary — and it challenges you to use your knowledge and abilities to write, speak, and gain recognition for the unique product you are marketing — *you*!

Imagine the possibilities: You, speaking with confidence at meetings, presenting information to senior executives, or as a keynote speaker at conferences. You, having your commentary and accomplishments published in the company newsletter or Ezine. You, the company spokesperson for print and broadcast media, an expert interviewed on radio and TV. You, the author of a book quoted in newspapers, and having articles published in magazines.

Hard to imagine? Then you really will be astonished when you follow through with this phase of my **MAGIC** formula and find yourself being recognized and respected in new and important ways.

Creating commentary is not the daunting task you may think; it is not a secret realm with doors that open only to the lucky. In this chapter, I will show you that the mystique surrounding commentary is not so mysterious. You will learn how to navigate your way strategically through the opportunities to create commentary. You can be one of the "lucky" ones who gets published, listened to, quoted, and interviewed.

Even if you shy away from the spotlight and don't wish to gain public exposure — or your company forbids it for whatever reason — you still need to get recognized within your company and/or industry. People listen to what experts say and read what they write. I will explore all levels of creating commentary in this chapter.

The Case for Commentary

Why is creating commentary so important?

Commentary provides visibility in a big — possibly huge — way. A 2003 study called "Women in U.S. Corporate Leadership," conducted by New York-based Catalyst, found that having a recognized expertise in a specific content area is one major way women succeeded in corporate leadership.

The Catalyst research also concludes that advancement, especially within larger organizations, is highly dependent on visibility — the fifth frequently cited finding in this area. The most frequently cited reason was exceeding performance expectations and successfully managing others (traits that would fall under the **M** and **I** in my **MAGIC** formula).

Catalyst President Ilene Lang stated, "We believe that companies need to give women high-visibility, high-impact career opportunities and support them in those assignments."

There seems no doubt that women who want to get ahead should put more effort into creating visibility for themselves.

"As a woman, it's very important to be out publicly speaking on issues that aren't just women's issues," said Gail Evans, former Executive Vice President, CNN News Group, and author of the book *She Wins, You Win.*

The problem is that at a very early age, many women got the idea that they weren't supposed to be outspoken. Therefore, women tend to understate their contributions and abilities. They want to be perfect, get it absolutely right, and think that they have to be the world's leading experts before they can seek visibility. The result? Many never get heard.

"Many women were not raised to promote or market themselves," said Molly D. Shepard, President and CEO of The Leader's Edge. "Women need to get in touch with what they've accomplished and tell people what they've done."

Certainly, what you do matters. But in business, what others see or perceive you do matters as much and sometimes more. And the more people who see you, the better! It's not enough to stand out within your company as a hardworking professional. Take your expertise and **MAGIC** out from behind the curtain and walk to the center of the stage. Let a wider circle of business professionals in your company and industry know what you are capable of doing.

"I did my writing and speaking within the company where I worked, and I now realize I should have used these communication skills to get visibility externally, too," said Dr. Catherine E. Palmier, Chief Medical Officer of United Healthcare of Georgia. "If I had, I would be more well known."

"It's important to get outside your company and create a persona of yourself so others talk about you," said Heidi Hunter, Vice President and Global Business Manager, Oncology for Wyeth. "Last year, I spoke at two industry conferences. These were opportunities for me to expand my visibility. People not only learned *from* me, they learned *about* me."

If the promise of greater visibility and career advancement doesn't get you moving, then think about job security! If things get tight in your organization, the first ones to be let go will be those who don't stand out and demonstrate the motivation necessary in tough times. Your visibility and commentary adds to your network of advocates — people who will help you find work when the chips are down. Your visibility also adds value as an employee. It may be just the edge you need when senior management has to "down size" or decide who gets ahead in the workplace and who gets left behind.

Commentary builds your status as an expert in your field. In order to really get recognition, you need to be considered an expert. People listen to experts. Experts are expected to create commentary. When you create commentary, you are showing the world that people in high places value your opinion and expertise enough to sponsor you as a speaker, to print what you write, to use you as a resource. You are also demonstrating that you have an audience who wants to read or listen to what you have to say. This helps validate the significance of your contributions.

Commentary is also tangible evidence that you possess qualities necessary for leadership roles and advancement. It shows that you have initiative, confidence and leadership skills. It shows that you are motivated: Through commentary, you are making the extra effort to express yourself in ways that many people don't even bother to attempt.

When people see or hear your commentary, they may be getting a first (and fabulous) impression of you. If they already know you, the fact that you create commentary will cause them to consider you with even greater regard. And if they had doubts about your abilities, they are likely to be won over by the motivation and expertise you demonstrate through your commentary.

Catherine J. Ross, President, Security Services for Day & Zimmermann, can recall an instance when commentary helped improve her interactions with the president of her company. "At the time, he didn't have a good impression of me. We didn't have a good relationship. Then, I invited him to attend a presentation I was giving. He must have been impressed, because after the presentation our relationship improved and he started saying nice things about me."

Never underestimate the impact your commentary can have beyond personal recognition.

Dr. Catherine A. Sohn, Vice President Worldwide Business Development, Consumer Healthcare at GlaxoSmithKline, was named "2003 Woman of the Year" by the Healthcare Businesswomen's Association (HBA). At her awards luncheon, she took the opportunity to bring attention to the debate surrounding prescription medicines. Dr. Sohn shared eye-opening statistics on the positive effects pharmaceuticals have on saving lives, improving quality of life, and reducing overall healthcare costs. In her commentary, she challenged all Healthcare Businesswomen's Association members to do a better job in communicating this message to the rest of the country.

When the media covered Dr. Sohn's receipt of this prestigious award, it was her commentary that received attention. By taking a stand on something important to her and the industry she serves, Dr. Sohn's commentary has resulted in ongoing recognition and attention far beyond her award.

Last, but not least, create commentary because it gives your life more meaning and makes you feel better about yourself! Your accomplishments in a new endeavor will raise your self-esteem, while making you more interesting and confident.

Commentary is something you can be proud of. Just think about it — potential local, national and international exposures as an industry expert; doesn't that sound great?

Creating commentary may be the last piece of my **MAGIC** formula, but it connects and positively impacts all the other pieces. Commentary is the edge you need to market yourself, develop advocates, grow and get involved — in a way that makes you feel good about who you are and what you do, and gets people to sit up and take notice!

So, What's Stopping You?

With so many good reasons to create commentary, why aren't more people doing it?

There are, as with so many of the other parts of the **MAGIC** formula, a few common excuses — but none of them are good! For instance ...

Rationalization #1: I don't know enough.

I thought we told that voice to be quiet in chapter one! If you think you are lacking in some way, then get the knowledge or information that will help. Interview people, read, take classes — grow! Talk to your mentors and the other people in your network. Creating commentary is the reason for growth, as well as the result of growth.

Your goal is to become an expert in your field so you are better able to help others. Once you're a recognized expert in your industry or role, you will be respected more by your peers and superiors. You also would have even more reason why a promotion and/or raise is warranted during your next review!

Rationalization #2: Writing, speaking, all that extra communicating ... it's too much work and I don't have the time.

I've covered this excuse before, haven't I? The ironic thing is, the extra work now can actually make life easier in the long run!

"If you don't write and speak, your progress will be slower," said Betty L. Siegel, Ph.D., President of Kennesaw State University in Kennesaw, Georgia.

What if your commentary leads to better opportunities, which might mean more income or less stress?

The answer to this rationalization is that commentary is important, so make the time for it.

Eliminate — don't just reduce — the time-wasting stuff in your life. Make a commitment and set a goal for creating commentary. Cut back a bit, and redirect your efforts to create the visibility that will really push you forward in your career. You will be so rewarded by what you can accomplish, you will want to make it an ongoing commitment.

Rationalization #3: What if I publicly humiliate myself?

What could you possibly do by creating commentary that you can't fix or recover from? Even if you do mishandle a question from a reporter, the potential embarrassment will be temporary — people will move on to the next thing in the news within minutes. Besides, if you prepare and practice, you won't humiliate yourself.

Think back to the discussion on taking risks in the chapter on growth. First, consider what the best possible outcome could be: By creating commentary, you can get maximum exposure and powerful visibility. Now, consider the worst possible outcome, and what you can do if the worst actually *did* happen. If you can get up and go on, then it's an intelligent, calculated risk worth taking.

Rationalization #4: Getting my name "out there" seems a bit too scary.

We all have fears. For many people, speaking in front of large groups is the number one panic inducer. So, most people are very understanding when it comes to stage fright. Your audience members are not your enemy. Most of them are not going to take the same effort to create commentary that you are making, and they will respect you for that. So overcome the timidity that bars you from opportunity. Do the thing that seems scary — that's what courage is all about! The next time, it will be easier.

Or, if possible, seek coaching or training to improve this important skill. A mentor who is experienced in this area could also assist in honing your presentation skills.

"At first, I was terrified about getting in front of people," said Evans, who is also author of *Play Like A Man Win Like A Woman.* "But I did it. It forced me to stretch."

Commentary Comes in All Shapes and Forms

Every time you write a memo, have a conversation, run a meeting or send an e-mail, you are creating commentary. Commentary always matters. Work on building your communication skills at a basic level, and you will feel more confident and competent when you go on to create commentary on more visible levels.

So where do you begin when you want to strategically communicate what you know? There are three initial steps:

Three-Pronged Approach to Strategic Communication

1.   Identify Your Area(s) of Expertise

Consider your field, your experience and credentials, and don't minimize what you have to offer. You need to select a topic that you can talk or write about confidently and expertly.

For example, I am a workplace/career expert with specific areas of focus on presentation skills, business etiquette and self-marketing strategies for career success. Since I've already written books in these areas of expertise, I can better position myself as an expert speaker in these subjects, and generate more media exposure as an author. What are *your* areas of expertise?

2.   Target Your Market

What audience is most important for your success? Make sure you can communicate your topic in a way that addresses their needs or appeals to their interests.

Here are some key possibilities you may choose to identify as your target market (audience):

- Your clients and prospects (get into industry magazines they read, and then send them "tearsheets" — copies — as FYI).

- Colleagues and senior executives in networking and trade associations (most groups have internal publications — get your name and accomplishments in them). These groups often have speakers educate their members during meetings and special events, and if you're willing to volunteer your services, they'll be thrilled to book you.

- Internally, within your company — especially senior management (consider writing for staff newsletters or industry journals they'll read)

- Your community (consider submitting letters to the editor of your hometown paper, or seek a profile as a local success story)

I'll delve more into the "where" of creating commentary later in this chapter.

3. Decide How to Reach Your Market

Decide what would be the best way to get your commentary across to the audience you have identified as your target market. Would speaking or writing be most effective? Or, would TV or radio exposure be more conducive?

One way to increase your exposure is to speak up more at meetings and write internal memos when warranted. Get your name known; don't just blend into the background.

What are you most comfortable with? What are the opportunities?

Create Commentary Through Speaking

Speaking during meetings, conferences or other company/industry events is an important way to expand your visibility and create the commentary that establishes your reputation as an expert. The goal with speaking is to get out there and give presentations until your name is synonymous with your subject.

These presentations could occur during meetings in the form of sharing sales figures, volunteering to update the team on various projects happening, etc. The point is you're making your presence known — it doesn't matter if it's a department meeting or a company-wide event, you are increasing your visibility by speaking.

Judith E. Tschirgi, Chief Information Officer & Senior Vice President, at SEI Investments, said, "Early in my career, during departmental meetings on affirmative action, I volunteered to give a talk. It went over well. Word of mouth spread, and I became in demand in other departments."

The same positive results from speaking are regularly obtained by Catherine A. Gretta, Corporate Vice-President, Women's Markets for New York Life Insurance Company. She said, "When I speak, I speak from the heart, which is why I need to deliver messages I believe in. This has helped me in developing great relationships with my audiences. Many members have told me they felt as though I was actually speaking to them and that I truly cared." Gretta added that speaking has given her "the opportunity to manage through people

Your Strategy

Decide how you want to be positioned as an expert resource:

_____

_____

Write down who your target audience will be:

_____

_____

Next, consider the best place, and the best way to reach this audience with your commentary. Would it be through speaking at a trade association meeting or conference? Writing an article for the company newsletter or a trade journal? List your ideas below:

_____

_____

at all levels within the organization." And she continued, "I have been told that I have the ability to connect with groups."

The goal with speaking is to get out there and give presentations until your name is synonymous with your subject.

"Find your voice and then use it," said Heidi Hunter, Vice President and Global Business Manager, Oncology, for Wyeth.

"Speaking is a critical factor to success," said Susan F. Ward, a Vice President at UPS. "To be able to speak in front of a large group, you must be able to speak with confidence."

Some people, especially women, are afraid to speak up for themselves and are reluctant to talk about accomplishments, even in small group discussions. As I have said before, this is precisely what holds many women back. So, overcome the timidity that bars you from opportunity. Do the thing that may seem scary — that's what courage is all about! The next time, it will be easier.

"People have to be courageous," said Jeanie Duck, Senior Vice President of The Boston Consulting Group. "Practice courage in everyday activities. Speak out at meetings. Learn to say, 'I deserve this money.' Say, 'I'm going to go for it, even if I don't know the answer now.' It helps with practice and accepting failure and preparing for the next time. Be willing to put yourself out there."

Speak up, and speak out — and do it often! In time, you may even learn to enjoy it!

Make Your Voice Heard Within Your Company

It is essential that you speak to others and groups within your company in order to be noticed and advance your career. There are many opportunities within your firm to make your voice heard.

Start on a small level and build your confidence. First, share your contributions and best practices with your managers and other advocates. This is the prelude to sharing your expertise with larger groups. It is an opportunity to take stock of what you know and practice your delivery. Give recognition to others in your company. Saying nice things about your advocates is a good way to reciprocate for the support they give you.

"Have open conversations with people about what you do," said Michelle A. Rosen, Senior Director Strategy, Business Development, at McDonald's Corporation. "Self promote by telling stories. Talk about other people's successes."

In your commentary, be matter-of-fact about your successes; don't act egotistical. The facts speak for themselves when your efforts are noteworthy.

"Show confidence, not arrogance," said Ellen Levine, Editor-in-Chief of *Good Housekeeping* magazine. "I notice people who can deliver a message, who can talk the talk and walk the walk."

Also, make sure you tell your managers and other advocates that you would like to develop your skills, and present to a larger group. Remember, they can help you accomplish this, but they are not mind readers. You have to let them know about your goals.

Company meetings are perfect opportunities for you to volunteer to speak. Give regular presentations to your staff. Ask to give presentations to various departments, or do "lunch and learn" sessions. The more you present, the more comfortable you will become. And, you'll be increasingly viewed as someone who can articulate the company vision — resulting in greater exposure and possible promotions.

"You need to be able to present at meetings with your staff; you need to be comfortable," Peggi Einhorn, Senior Vice President at JPMorganChase. "Communication skills are highly important."

If you don't feel ready to take a role leading or presenting at meetings, offer to introduce the speaker. This is a good way to get comfortable with your public speaking voice and persona. Be sure to contribute verbally within the first 10 minutes of a meeting, even if your contribution is simply to support someone else. This can be the prelude to sharing your expertise on a wider scale. It is an opportunity to take stock of what you know and hone your delivery.

Consider donating your time as a speaker to local high schools and colleges. They will be thrilled to have a local business expert help educate their students.

Your involvements also provide plenty of opportunities for public speaking. Here are some examples:

- Present the results of a task force or committee to senior management.

- Offer to present at a monthly trade association meeting.

- Speak at the PTA meeting.

- If you are a director within an association, you will probably have the opportunity to introduce conference speakers, lead workshops, give welcome messages, etc.

- Teach a course at a local community college or high school.

Sheryl Craun, Vice President of Client Services, ADP Retirement Services, has spoken at church conferences, women's groups and college classes. "It's helped market me on my resume," she said. "Speaking in my community has exposed me to people I wouldn't have otherwise met, and given me job opportunities. I've also been a paid speaker, which demonstrates I have value."

"I've gotten lots of recognition by speaking through industry organizations and within the community," said Janice Price, President and CEO of The Kimmel Center for the Performing Arts.

If you don't like to speak, you can learn. This goes back to growth. Take a public speaking course. Get a speech coach. Join Toastmasters (www.toastmasters.org). Start small until you gain your skill and your confidence. In time, you may even learn to like it!

Start your plan to create commentary through speaking:

List three to five topics you can speak confidently and competently about:

_____

_____

_____

List opportunities for speaking in front of groups about these topics:

_____

_____

_____

Commit to a timetable for when you will give your first presentation on any of these topics:

_____

_____

_____

Create Commentary Through Writing

A sure way to become known as an expert is to write and then get published.

If you need to sharpen your writing skills, remember that my **MAGIC** formula involves growth! To grow as a writer, read publications and study good writing styles. Keep files of the best material, especially articles that relate to your area(s) of expertise. Refer to these articles for a jumpstart when you've got a case of writer's block.

Take a writing class at your community college. If your company's training department offers a writing program, sign up. Practice writing. Write within your company, and remember to craft all your documents carefully. Just as there are no unimportant people, there are no unimportant forms of communication. Your memos, letters and e-mails can add to, or detract from, your personal image.

Use your writing skills to become visible and appreciated within your company — don't be afraid to share your "two cents." Volunteer to help edit the writing of others.

"I have good writing skills, which has been an asset in expanding my visibility," said Margery Geers, Vice President, Human Resources, Healthcare Management Services, of Aramark Corp. "I've been asked to review other people's materials and got recognition for knowing how to write."

Create commentary about yourself, your team and your successes on a regular basis — keeping managers and others informed of your efforts.

"You've got to remind people of what you accomplish," said Peggi Einhorn, Senior Vice President at JPMorganChase. "I do this with a monthly update on accomplishments with my manager, mostly in memo form. I also write a quarterly summarization that informs people about what I do, as well as what others on my team have done."

It doesn't matter if your writing appears within your company or in the public domain — locally or nationally — the more exposure, the better. You never know who will be reading your memo, article or letter to the editor.

Submit Commentary to Newsletters/Ezines

Newsletters, and their digital counterparts, Ezines, are a great way to create written commentary. The people who produce these publications are usually eager for a copy and will welcome your submissions. Your company and trade association newsletters/Ezines are good choices. Contact clients and submit articles to their trade association journals, corporate newsletters, etc.

Get to know the people who produce internal publications and find out how to contribute commentary. Submit information on your achievements, best practices, team efforts, task forces, media exposure, etc.

"There are monthly highlights and quarterly reports that get submitted, and you must get your project in these to get company recognition," explained Dr. Catherine A. Sohn, Vice President Worldwide Business Development, Consumer Healthcare at GlaxoSmithKline. She did this by talking to corporate communications and asking how they decide what goes into quarterly reports. "Then, figure out how your product or your team's success and initiatives can be included," she said. "This gets recognition for your team as well as for you."

Cheryl Doll, Vice President of Marketing and Planning of LodgeWorks, said, "I do an internal news release, and the focus is on the new people in the company. I've gotten publicity and recognition from that. The idea is that by promoting others, you will promote yourself."

If you are an entrepreneur, consider publishing your own newsletter or Ezine. Even a one-page newsletter can be an effective way to market yourself and your services. You can print your newsletter in-house or through a local printer, depending on your budget. You can also e-mail it to clients and prospects on a regular basis.

My company, Brody Communications Ltd., has a free, quarterly newsletter that people can subscribe to on our Web site (www.BrodyCommunications.com). It's a way of creating value and visibility.

Newspapers: Another Place for Commentary

Write letters to the editor at local and national newspapers. This will give you visibility as you improve your writing skills. A letter to the editor requires a concise style that effectively conveys your viewpoint about a current event or topic of interest. It's the perfect exercise for writers!

Submit a piece for the Op-Ed (short for Opposite the Editorial) section of a newspaper. Include a cover letter to the editor giving your credentials and your phone number.

If you enjoy writing and can make the commitment, offer to write a column for your local newspaper. Keep in mind that there will be deadlines, probably on a weekly basis.

There also are numerous newsletters published nationally on a wide range of business topics geared to the working professional. Target these publications for your commentary as well. Find those that focus on your industry and/or types of companies.

Magazines

There are thousands of trade and consumer magazines in existence. And a large percentage regularly seek "freelance" or outside contributions from nonstaff members.

Find out what magazines your target market reads and get your articles published in them. A good type of article for this purpose is the "How To" article. It gives you a chance to share your best practices and highlight your expertise.

Doing a quick "Google" search on the Internet (www.Google.com) can help you find the magazines to target. You can also buy the most recent version of *Writer's Market*, which lists publications and their editorial submission policies.

If your area of expertise would fit well with a trade publication, contact the editor to see if he or she would like your articles. For example, I don't submit my business and corporate communication-themed pieces to *Golf Digest*.

Karen Daroff, President of Daroff Design Inc., a Philadelphia-based full service architecture & interior design firm, was published in *Interior Design* magazine. She went to see the editor, and showed him her work from Cobblestones Restaurant. At that point she didn't even have a subscription to the magazine! The result of her meeting? The editor published her work. "He said I had chutzpah," said Daroff.

Choose 10 to 25 publications that can work for you, and write and send articles to them regularly. All submissions should be accompanied by biographical information so you get proper credit when the articles are published. This "credit blurb" needs to also have your contact information (phone number, Web site, e-mail address, etc.).

Also, always offer to send a color or black-and-white headshot photo. Many magazines like to feature pictures of their special contributors.

After you find a match for your target market and potential topic, write a query letter or e-mail to the editor or managing editor (try to find out which form of communication he or she prefers). This letter should be brief, less than one full page. In the first paragraph of the letter, describe what the potential article is about. In the second paragraph, explain why it would be interesting or informative to the publication's readers. In the third paragraph, tell why you are qualified to write about the topic. Consider sending a draft of your article as FYI — or at least a few bullet points from it.

Send your query letter to the editor along with a self-addressed, stamped envelope. If you are writing for income, don't send the article, however, until you get a favorable reply. Always include a copyright line in your article indicating that you own the rights to your work, and that permission must be granted to reproduce it in any form. If you're being paid for a submission, you can then negotiate these rights.

If you hate to write or for whatever reason choose not to, volunteer to be quoted as an expert for articles.

Of course, whenever you have something published, make your advocates aware of it. Always get tear sheets (copies of articles you've had published) from the publisher. You also may be able to get copies of the actual magazine itself. Send copies of your work in print to clients and advocates, enhancing your visibility and credentials as an expert.

Become an Author — Write a Book!

In time, you might find you like writing so much that you can write a book about your area of expertise. Writing a book, while more involved than writing an article, can reap huge rewards. The phrase "published author" before or after your name can open many doors (i.e., get new clients and business), and also lead to further media exposure.

Writing a book does not have to be an onerous task. You don't have to do it alone. Get a writing partner or co-author. Six of my 18 books were co-authored. The advantage of this is sharing responsibility and fun in collaboration. Working with a ghostwriter is another option. It can be costly, but it gets the job done. Get a good editor. If possible, use your company's communication department for editing.

To begin the process of writing a book, first determine your PAL™ — Purpose, Audience, and Logistics:

> Purpose — What do you want to achieve?
> Audience — What target market is most
> important for your success?
> Logistics — How long will the book be,
> how many chapters, etc.

Sample Query Letter

Dear (Editor),

Good morning!

Would you be interested in an article I've written titled "How to Write Better Business Letters?"

My article focuses on common mistakes executives often make when writing. It gives ideas for writing letters that are professional and easy to understand. The article also shows how to improve your image through your business writing.

I have been the vice president of communications for XYZ Corporation for the past 10 years, where I am responsible for writing and editing all training manuals and corporate communications. I also run several executive writing programs within our organization.

I will be in touch with you later this month to answer your questions about the attached draft and discuss in which issue it could fit.

Thank you for your consideration.

Sincerely,

Enclosure

Then, brainstorm ideas and cluster them into chapters or segments. If you have written articles, you could possibly combine them into chapters.

Once you have your chapters outlined, the next step is to do research. Citing statistics or other industry studies always adds to your book's value as a resource. If possible, consider doing your own surveys and using the results.

At this point in the process, write the first draft, give it to others for feedback, then do any rewrites and have it edited. It is a back-and-forth process.

If you hate to write, you can still get published. Offer your expertise and quotes to noncompeting colleagues who are writing books. Being included in their books adds leverage to your expert status without the longer commitment required to write a book of your own.

Writing for Web Sites — Yours & Others

If you are an entrepreneur, having a Web site is an essential marketing strategy and a place to create commentary. Regularly update all articles on your site to drive return traffic.

Remember, people can't visit your site unless they are aware of it. Once your page is ready, e-mail all the search engines with the key words related to your site so people who "surf" the Web can find you. It also is an excellent way for members of the media to find you. I also list on my Web site the most recent and impressive places where my work has appeared — or where I've been quoted.

Contact noncompeting colleagues. See if they would like to link their pages to yours. You can also contact sites related to your area of expertise to investigate link possibilities.

Another way to use the Internet for commentary is to submit articles to Web sites and get profiled on "expert pages" and sites related to your area of expertise. Sometimes there may be a nominal fee, but it may pay off in exposure. Some sites, like print publications, will also pay you for articles to post.

Create Commentary Through Media Exposure

Getting editorial exposure through newspapers, radio and television is better than advertising. It establishes you as being credible and endorsed by the media in which your commentary appears.

And, if you hate writing, position yourself as an expert to contact by virtue of your many years of industry expertise (if appropriate). The more quotes and on-camera/on-air time you get as a result, the higher your media value will be in the future — and the more highly sought after media expert you become.

Cultivate relationships with the media in order to establish yourself as an expert they can contact when they need quotes, an interview, or a source. Position yourself so you are seen as your company's spokesperson.

Take the initiative to send news releases, photos and media kits to newspapers, radio and television. Learn how to give a good interview.

Start your plan to create commentary through writing:

List three to five topics you can write about:

_____

_____

_____

List where you could have this writing published:

_____

_____

_____

Commit to a timetable for when you will write your first article, letter to the editor, etc.:

_____

_____

_____

PR is Paramount

Make sure you send out news releases to all media — radio, TV and print — whenever you reach a milestone

Sample News Release

FOR IMMEDIATE RELEASE

Contact: Miryam S. Roddy
215-886-1688
mroddy@BrodyCommunications.com

Next Month, Mind your Manners! Everybody Is Watching

Jenkintown, PA — *Chase's Calendar of Events* declares August 2003 **National Win with Civility Month**. When dealing with clients, common courtesy is as important as the quality of product being sold. When dealing with co-workers lack of it could cost one a promotion or even their job! The Research Institute of America reported that 96 percent of customers never complain about discourteous professionals, but 91 percent specifically decide *not to do business with companies who have in some way offended them*. A recent study also found that 6 out of 10 people said their colleagues never said "good morning" to them.

According to Chase, "When we are civil to each other we confirm our worth and acknowledge the worth of others." Workplace/career expert Marjorie Brody agrees wholeheartedly and offers the following two areas for professionals to remember to practice proper office civility:

1. Watch basic manners
   - Say "please" and "thank you," "hello" and "goodbye"
   - Open doors (regardless of gender)
   - Write thank-you notes
2. Maintain a professional appearance
   - Business casual doesn't mean sloppy; remember that clothing creates an impression
   - Don't wear cologne that is too strong
   - Watch your language
   - Be aware of slang and avoid foul language and sarcasm
   - Power robbers ("I hope," "I guess," "maybe," "probably") undercut one's credibility

Brody is co-author of the award-winning book *Help! Was That a Career Limiting Move?* and author of *21st Century Pocket Guide to Proper Business Protocol*.

She is founder and fearless leader of Brody Communications Ltd., where she helps individuals achieve their potential by strengthening their professionalism, persuasiveness and presence. Brody has presented to more than 2,000 audiences, and has appeared on CNBC, Fox-TV, Oxygen Network, and been quoted in *The Wall Street Journal, Cosmopolitan, Washington Post, People, Business Week, Glamour, Fortune* and in many other national publications. To schedule an interview, contact Miryam S. Roddy at 800-726-7936.

-30-

(such as a company anniversary), receive an award, open a new office, publish a new book, etc.

Use letterhead, and keep it to one page, double spaced if possible. Get the main facts in the first and second paragraphs, reporter style: listing the who, what, when, where, why, and how. The first paragraph should be about three sentences, no more than five lines long.

Include at least one quote from you, or the company Chairman, CEO or President (if that's not already you). It usually works well if you start off the second paragraph with a quote.

As you write the rest of the release, keep in mind that editors may omit copy for space. So get the important details in at the beginning, and don't be surprised if the information in your last paragraph never makes it to the actual story.

The better the news release, the less work for a harried editor on deadline, and the more likely your story will get printed — possibly just the way you've written it. A good photograph increases your chances of being published. Send it to the appropriate editor. Make sure that you include all contact information.

Send Media Kits

Always make sure you have a media kit ready to send out at a moment's notice. This includes a color photograph of yourself (but also have a black-and-white photo ready if it's specially requested), your biography, company profile, client list, articles about you and your company, references and recommendation letters. Put it all in a folder with your business card. You can have special, imprinted folders designed for this purpose, or make your own by putting a label on the front.

Send this kit with a cover letter when there's a good connection for your area of expertise — an event in the news and/or a seasonal angle. For example, December is a good time to pitch a piece on business gift giving etiquette — a tie-in that's landed me national exposure many times.

Get on radio and TV talk shows and other programs as a guest to address a specific topic or to talk about your newest book. Start small, with a local university radio station, or a local or cable stations. You never know who may be listening or watching.

Be Attuned to Radio Appearance Possibilities

You also can create commentary by being a guest on radio shows. Radio provides excellent exposure, whether it's AM news or talk shows (for a more serious segment) or FM programs featuring music and deejays (where a more fun piece is possible). For example, *Chase's Calendar of Events* allows me to have humorous tie-ins with business etiquette issues. I was a guest on many FM morning radio programs when Chase's said July 2003 was "National Cell Phone Courtesy Month" — my PR staff made sure the media knew I was a great etiquette expert that could be contacted for my "two cents" on this issue.

Start by listening to radio stations to determine which would be appropriate for your message and would enable you to reach your target market. Pay attention to each show's format and the host's interview style. You may want to get initial experience through a local or college station. Eventually, you may want to get on syndicated shows for maximum radio exposure — these programs air in many markets across the country.

Next, decide how you could contribute as a guest on the show. Adapt your message for the broadcast style of commentary. Focus on a few key points to emphasize. Work on your delivery. Be enthusiastic; speak in short sentences. Remember the verbal and vocal points I shared in the chapter on Manner as you practice.

Find out the name of the show's producer and let this person know you would like to appear as a guest. Then send any releases or media kits to him or her.

When it's time for your interview, bring media reminder cards. These are index cards listing all your contact information (name, phone numbers, Web site, etc.) and book details, which you can give to the host(s) and producer so they have your pertinent information at a glance when listeners call in. During the show, or after the program, you can offer something to listeners, like a free brochure or book, which they can request by calling in or sending their name and address.

As an alternative to giving your radio interview at the station in a studio, it's possible to be interviewed by telephone. Ask for this option if it would make you feel less nervous, or if the show time and location pose logistical difficulties.

Smile, You're on TV!

Always have an ample supply of media kits and news releases to send all local TV stations. Again, these would be sent with appropriate PR "pitches" for them to book you as the expert source.

Also, strive to become known as your company's spokesperson. Be prepared to give an interview that is appropriate for television. This means being ready to give the sound bites a reporter needs to do a compelling story. Think of a snappy, powerful way to summarize your topic in one or two sentences. Go back to the **M** part of my **MAGIC** formula and look, speak and present your professional best. Stand straight, holding your head straight. The camera will love you!

Go For It & Then Keep Going!

The goal with commentary is to keep you in front of the audience that you have determined is important for your success. If you're waiting around for an invitation to get this kind of recognition and credibility, you may wait forever. Make creating commentary part of your strategic plan and start today. This is how you become the expert with maximum exposure, the professional with powerful visibility.

Once you start to create commentary, keep going — and growing. Do bigger and better types of commentary as you gain experience and skill. Start by targeting local, then aim for the national media.

"Even at a high level, you must maintain high visibility," said Cheryl Doll, Vice President of Marketing and Planning, LodgeWorks.

Stay visible. Never stop creating commentary!

Chapter 7
Go Work Your MAGIC!

Turn Your Life Into a Masterpiece

My goal for this book was to give you a tool to help you discover the magic within. At this point, resolve that you will no longer view life from the sidelines, accept or create limitations for yourself. You are moving toward the career you desire, getting noticed for your contributions and creating opportunities. You know the **MAGIC** formula. Now keep going and keep growing.

Be determined to turn your life into a masterpiece!

This point struck me while I was doing needlepoint on a recent airplane flight. Needlepoint is a favorite hobby of mine. It enables me to relax, helps pass the time while I travel, and also provides a way for me to make special gifts for the people I care about. I am always thrilled to see how the hundreds of stitches eventually come together and form the picture I had envisioned when I began.

On that recent plane trip, I was happy that I would soon complete the project I was working on, and get it upholstered for a footstool for my youngest daughter. I had filled the front quite nicely with colorful and even stitches.

I turned the scrim over to cut a loose end, and the reverse side wasn't perfect. Yet, the stitches would hold firm, they would never unravel, and the way they looked did not detract from the lovely details on the front — no one would ever see the back since it would be on a footstool. I would have the project done in time for my daughter's birthday and she would love it. It was a gift of my time and talents and it came from my heart. I could have made the reverse side look neater, more precise, and even perfect, but it would have taken at least twice as much time and energy — and it wouldn't have mattered.

I realized that the needlepoint is a metaphor for how I have achieved goals in my life! I advise you to take a similar approach: Use your talents to make something wonderful and beautiful out of your life, something that will last and have meaning. Do not waste time and effort on invisible and unimportant details. Focus on what matters. Do what needs to be done as well as you can, accept that some of it will not be perfect and doesn't need to be. Take risks, grow, and be visible in positive ways.

Excelling in your job and having a positive work ethic is the foundation for advancement in your career. Build on that foundation in order to get promoted, rewarded and paid what you're worth. Simply being a good, hard worker is not enough. Taking the **MAGIC** steps that I presented in this book will help you get the recognition that you deserve.

In my experience as an executive coach, I've found that many women block *themselves* from reaching their potential. Without realizing it, they make choices that are self-defeating. They direct too much time and effort into tasks that don't get noticed. I work with these women to focus on the big picture — the masterpiece they want to create of their lives — and to let go of the self-limiting attitudes and approaches holding them back.

In this book, I've given you the tools and techniques to get unblocked and make your career yet another part of your life that is well lived and fully enjoyed. These strategies don't cost money and they are not a waste of time. Use them! And as you do, let go of perfection; work on success and getting results instead. In the quest for perfection, you don't get as much done and your life can be unnecessarily stressful.

Focus on what you really want. What are you looking for in your career? Where would you like to see yourself in one year? Five years? Ten years?

Next, look at the action steps — all the parts of my **MAGIC** formula — necessary to get there. What do you need to do? If you have a goal that seems overwhelming (and the big, most worthwhile goals often do seem this way at first), break it into pieces. When you turn it into a series of smaller goals, it's easier to get started and keep going. If you take this approach, and you are determined and motivated, you can do almost anything.

Once you know where you want to go and you've defined the possibilities and actions to take, consider what barriers you face and how to overcome each one.

Finally, it's a matter of putting the plan into action. In almost all cases, getting positive recognition for your current work contributions and career actions will help you achieve whatever goals you have.

Many people intuitively do what I've talked about. Perhaps you've recognized yourself already doing some of the things I've recommended in the **MAGIC** formula. This is good, but it may not be enough. Make strategic choices or your career path may be without direction, like a leaf blowing in the wind. Of course, always be open to options and opportunities along the way.

Create choices. Create maximum visibility. Never stop learning, and growing and using your **MAGIC**. It's been inside you all along!

Chapter 8
What Others Are Doing

Brody Communications Ltd. surveyed 308 professionals in the fall of 2002 from a variety of industries, including financial, government, banking, travel, pharmaceuticals, beverage, aerospace, computer, defense, engineering and manufacturing. Of those surveyed, 171 were women and 137 were men.

Here are some of the women's personal marketing ideas:

Idea (age/industry)

- Set up weekly update meeting with my line manager to tell him what I've done (22, pharmaceutical)
- Stop by boss' office every day, uninvited (22, financial)
- Introduce myself to senior execs when appropriate (22, banking)
- Participate in the firm's mentoring program (35, defense)
- Say "hello" and introduce myself to everyone (47, pharmaceutical)
- Networking (22, financial)
- Get to know at least one personal thing about everyone — talk to people, ask questions (42, financial)

What Others Are Doing

- Meet people from other departments to learn what they do and let them know who I am (26, travel)

- Going back to school (age not given, pharmaceutical)

- Keep up-to-date with current trends in technology (30, financial)

- Taking as many courses as I possibly can to help develop personally and professionally (33, pharmaceutical)

- Persuaded agency administration to reimburse tuition for master's degree program (47, government)

- Take in-house career classes and talk to HR and career contacts (50, computer)

- Attend professional conferences/meetings in my field (age not given, government)

- Getting involved in projects with various managers, instead of only working for myself (22, banking)

- Placing myself in positions to be seen and shine; willing to relocate for a certain position (25, pharmaceutical)

- Volunteer for projects/presentations (27, financial)

- Volunteering to help plan and organize the annual management conference (29, government)

- I founded a local chapter of a national, nonprofit, professional organization (30, pharmaceutical)

- Getting involved with team meetings (30, pharmaceutical)

- Joining Toastmasters, continuing with it, and initiating a team off-site for company (30, pharmaceutical)

- Attending conference in my field and industry (45, pharmaceutical)
- Involvement with a team that interacts with senior management (37, pharmaceutical)
- Volunteering for a difficult project (35, computer)
- Volunteer for "extra duties" representing our department in workshops and at seminars (age not given, government)
- Asked to be involved in other team meetings and agendas and give presentations (age not given, pharmaceutical)
- Clearly communicating accomplishments to management via writing each month (26, financial)
- Bringing up items that I've researched at team/department meetings (26, financial)
- Visiting another department and explaining what my department does (36, financial)
- Agreed to be featured in a national magazine when asked (43, pharmaceutical)
- Update manager on plans/accomplishments without being elicited (47, pharmaceutical)
- Wrote an article for bureau newsletter (57, government)
- Recent article in company newsletter promoting department and self in "career development" (age not given, pharmaceutical)
- Going to meetings, making presentations, publishing reports (30, pharmaceutical)
- Setting up and attending weekly meetings to convey current responsibilities (22, banking)

Chapter 9
Women Who've Blazed the Way

Debra Brown-Spruill, Executive Director, OCLC — Public Affairs
Information Service

Pearl of Wisdom: "Always make plans — for work, for life, for family — but use pencil instead of ink. This will help you keep your options open and enhance your flexibility."

STATS

Personal: Married, no children except their "whacky dog, Satchmo, a spoiled Akita"

Education: BA, Sociology, Douglass College; MLS, Library Science, Rutgers University

Business Background & Areas of Involvement

- Previously owned consulting firm for eight years, dataBase-Systems, specializing in electronic development and database design.
- National Federation of Abstracting and Indexing Services (Copyright Committee); Information Industry Association, Database Publication Division; Book Industry Advisory Group (Title Update Committee); American Society of Information Science; Kean College of New Jersey.
- New Jersey Council for the Humanities (chair); The Newark Museum Volunteer Organization (president & docent); The Bibliophiles — an African-American Reading Group; and Delta Sigma Theta sorority.
- Publications include "PAIS Prepares for the 21st Century," NFAIS Newsletter, October 1998; and "Impacts of Changing Production Technologies," Part 3, 1994 NFAIS Report Series, May 1995; Debra has spoken at numerous professional organizations.

Roslyn "Roz" Courtney, Managing Director, Roslyn Courtney Consulting

 Pearl of Wisdom: "We can all be leaders and agents of change at any stage in our career. Important achievements come from big ideas, our willingness to take on personal risks, our abilities to create a shared vision of success, and the involvement, contributions and support of others."

STATS

Personal: married, one child

Education: MBA, Strategic Management, The Wharton School; BA, Magna Cum Laude, Penn State University

Business Background & Areas of Involvement

- Previously served as a leader in creating successful human resource change globally for companies such as Kraft General Foods, The New York Times Company, The Citigroup Private Bank, and Primedia's Consumer Media and Magazine Group.
- International Association of Corporate and Professional Recruitment, New York Chapter (President, 1995-1998); Co-chair of a global Wharton Women's Initiative "to advance, develop and support women's leadership at all life stages," both within the Wharton community and in the broader business arena.
- In May 2002, Courtney launched a study of Exemplary Women Leaders for a Conference at the Wharton School to identify how these exceptional women drive their business and career successes. "Exemplary Leaders" has become an ongoing initiative of customized workshops, assessment and coaching programs to advance the leadership and results of individuals and teams.
- Courtney has published articles and has spoken as an authority on strategic change and leadership at numerous university, professional and industry programs.

Sheryl B. Craun, Vice President of Client Services, ADP Retirement Services (ADPRS)

Pearl of Wisdom: "Don't allow your fears to limit your potential or color other's perceptions of your ability. Create your own success!"

STATS

Personal: Married, two children

Education: BA, Psychology, Messiah College; two years of coursework at Temple University; currently working on a Master's in Financial Planning through the College for Financial Planning

Business Background & Areas of Involvement

- Previously directed shareholder relations for Geriatric and Medical Centers; a Principal with the Vanguard Group, serving many roles in the 16 years, most notably doing an office startup in Charlotte, NC, and growing the business.
- Has Series 7 and 24 Securities Licenses; certified in the Myers-Briggs instrument; certified as a Master Trainer through the AchieveGlobal organization.
- United Way Business Volunteers Council; Junior Achievement; Charlotte Executive Customer Care Council; National Association for Female Executives; and the American Society for Training and Development.

Jeanie Daniel Duck, Senior Vice President, The Boston Consulting Group

Pearl of Wisdom: "A good principle to live by is to 'be externally concerned and internally aware.' We usually do better when we are concerned for and connected with other people — whether they are coworkers, a team, or our communities. We need 'external concern,' because when we're only out for our own agenda, we are likely to have a skewered perspective, see the problems and opportunities too narrowly, miss the point entirely, and come across not only as self-centered, but untrustworthy."

STATS

Personal: Married, one child, two stepchildren

Education: MS, Art Education, Pratt Institute, New York; BS, University of Georgia

Business Background & Areas of Involvement

- Previously, Vice President of AmSouth Bank, Birmingham, AL; owned consulting firm in Minneapolis for eight years, consulting with a variety of businesses ranging from health care to large manufacturing companies and financial service firms.
- Duck taught figure drawing at the University of Alabama, Birmingham, and at Pratt Institute in New York.
- Planned Parenthood/Chicago Area (past board member).
- Author of *The Change Monster: The Human Forces that Fuel or Foil Corporate Transformation and Change*(Crown Business 2001), which has been translated into nine languages; author of many articles, including "Managing Change the Art of Balancing," *Harvard Business Review* 1991 (their best-selling reprint and included in *HBR on Change*).
- April 2003, featured on cover of *Consultants News* magazine.

Karen Daroff, President & Principal, Daroff Design

 Pearl of Wisdom: "Focus on the win, hold onto your values, and then be sure to research and explore all resources, contacts and talent to understand and connect with your client."

STATS

Personal: Married, one child, two stepchildren

Education: BFA, Interior Design, Moore College of Art

Business Background & Areas of Involvement

- Founded Daroff Design in 1973.
- Named by *Interiors* magazine as the 1990 Designer of the Year; one of Pennsylvania's "Best 50 Women in Business;" the 1999 "Women of Distinction" award by *Philadelphia Business Journal*.
- Greater Philadelphia Chamber of Commerce Board of Managers (board member); member of the Urban Land Institute, IAPPA, member, Network of Executive Women in Hospitality; Philadelphia Chapter of American Institute of Architects (Associate Member); University of the Arts in Philadelphia (Board of Trustees member).
- Guest speaker for the Harvard University Graduate School of Architecture's special lecture series, and has presented keynote addresses for many national industry events, including the annual national convention for interior designers and architects (NEOCON X), the National Buildings Show, the International Facilities Exposition, and the Milliken Hospitality Conference. She was also a featured speaker at the 1999 Rotterdam International Film Festival.
- Daroff has been published in many magazines, including: *Interior Design, Progressive Architecture, Architecture, Hospitality Design, Restaurant Business, Restaurant & Hotel Design International, Corporate Design, Casino Player, Nation's Restaurants News, Visual Merchandising and Store Design*, in addition to many local and regional publications. *AT Architecture, Pronto* and *Offica* — Japanese magazines — also have published her work. She also has been featured in many books on the design profession.

Cheryl Doll, Vice President of Marketing and Planning, Lodgeworks

Pearl of Wisdom: "I've tried playing by the rules and working the system, but real success, joy and meaning found me when I learned to be true to myself and God. Proverbs says, 'The one who blesses others is abundantly blessed; those who help others are helped.' It's not always the obvious path or easy to do, but it's made for a much richer journey."

STATS
Personal: Single
Education: BA, Magna Cum Laude, Journalism & Gore Leadership Scholar, Wichita State University

Business Background & Areas of Involvement
- Previously Vice President of Marketing & Communication at the All-Suites Division of Wyndham International in charge of brand marketing for Summerfield and Sierra Suites Hotels.
- Favorite involvements include: National Multiple Sclerosis Society; Wichita State University; YWCA Women's Safe House; Big Brothers & Big Sisters.
- Active member of Christ Episcopal Church, committees and programs (40 Days of Purpose outreach, Garden Walk, Missions' Auction, Youth Ministry, Small Groups).

Peggi Einhorn, Senior Vice President, JPMorganChase

Pearl of Wisdom: "Stay flexible. And always strive for balance in your life. You can't be successful without it."

STATS

Personal: Married, two children

Education: MBA, Finance and Marketing, Columbia University Graduate School of Business; B.A., Art History, William Smith College

Business Background & Areas of Involvement

- Previously worked for several art organizations, including The Jewish Museum, the Metropolitan Museum of Art, and the National Endowment for the Arts.
- 1999 recipient of a David Rockefeller Fellowship from the New York City Partnership.
- Board of the Brooklyn Children's Museum (past Chairman and ongoing Trustee).

Gail Evans, Former Executive Vice President, CNN News Group

 Pearl of Wisdom: "The era of 'I can do it' is coming to a close. Women must now think of entering the era of 'we can do it.' Isolated successes will not make women equal players in the world of business, only a collective effort will get us to the next level. We must begin to understand that for everyone who succeeds in business, 'I succeed,' and for every woman who fails, 'I fail.' We are viewed as a group and, therefore, we need to learn the power of the group and play like a team."

STATS

Personal: Divorced, three children; grandmother of five

Education: BA, Political Science, Bennington College

Business Background & Areas of Involvement

- Evans began her career in the early 1960s, when she worked on Capitol Hill as a legislative aide to Congressmen William Fitts Ryan and James Roosevelt; she then worked at the White House in the Office of the Special Counsel to the President during the Lyndon B. Johnson Administration. Evans worked on the creation of the president's Committee on Equal Employment Opportunity and the 1966 Civil Rights Act.
- Served as a member of CNN Executive Committee; CNN programming task force (chairperson).
- DuPree School of Management at Georgia Tech University (visiting professor); McColl/Garella Partners (board member); member, International Women's Forum, Committee of 200, and the Council on Foreign Relations.
- Active in Atlanta and Georgia charities, including: Kennesaw State University (Board of Trustees); Georgia State University School of Law (Board of Visitors); member, Citizens Review Panel of the Juvenile Court of Atlanta; Society for Women's Health Research (board member); Atlanta Girls School (board member).
- Has weekly syndicated radio segment "It's not Just A Man's World," available to 1,900 CNN radio affiliates throughout the U.S.; author of *Play Like A Man Win Like A Woman*, which has been translated into 18 languages. Her latest book is *She Wins, You Win*.

Suzanne F. Fairlie, CPC, President, ProSearch, Inc.

Pearl of Wisdom: "The glass half full is so much easier to look at and drink than the glass half empty."

STATS

Personal: Married, two children; one grandchild so far

Education: BA Mathematics, Gettysburg College

Business Background & Areas of Involvement

- Previously in Information Systems Management, working for IBM, Tandem, and Sun Oil.
- ProSearch was identified as one of the Top 10 search firms in Philadelphia by *The Philadelphia Business Journal*.
- Inducted to the Pennsylvania Honor Roll of Women; named by *Business Philadelphia* as one of the "Top 100 People to Watch"; provided expert witness testimony in employment issues; appeared on CNN, WCAU-TV Channel 10, and local radio and TV business and news shows.
- Member, Society for Information Management; member, The Forum of Executive Women; member, Union League of Philadelphia; U.S. Women's Chamber of Commerce (Vice President); National Association of Personnel Services (board of directors); Mid-Atlantic Association of Personnel Consultants (Government Affairs Chair and Ethics Chair); Pinnacle Society (board of directors).
- Junior Achievement of Delaware Valley (board of directors); La Salle University (Information Systems Advisory Board); Kutztown University (MIS Advisory Board); Society for Information Management (Program and Membership Committees); CIO Forum (Executive Advisory Board).
- Frequently been invited as a trainer in recruiting to various state and national associations and large national recruitment firms.

Margery Geers, Vice President, Human Resources, Healthcare Management Services, Aramark Corp.

Pearl of Wisdom: "If you don't believe in yourself, nobody else will. Self-confidence is the key to success."

STATS

Personal: Married, one daughter

Education: BS, Business Logistics, Penn State University

Business Background & Areas of Involvement

- Previously, she was Vice President of Human Resources for SAP America.
- Member, Society for Human Resource Management and Corporate Leadership Council.
- Involved in several national Charitable organizations centered around helping animals as well as people with disabilities.

Judith Giordan, Ph.D., Principal & Co-Founder, Aileron Partners; Director, ICMB Ocean Tomo

Pearl of Wisdom: "Remember, you're the CEO of Me.life! So be the creator of your career and your life — build your brand, let your life and career organically evolve together and, to paraphrase, always remember that a woman's (your) worth is far beyond rubies! So have passion and never settle for less than what you know you are worth."

STATS

Personal: Married, two stepchildren

Education: BS, Summa Cum Laude, Rutgers University; Ph.D., Physical Organic Chemistry, University of Maryland; Alexander von Humboldt Post Doctoral Research Fellow, University of Frankfurt in Germany.

Business Background & Areas of Involvement

- Previously held positions include Vice President — Director of R&D, International Flavors and Fragrances, Inc.; Vice President Global R&D, Pepsi-Cola Company; Vice President Research and Development, Henkel Corporation.
- American Chemical Society (Board of Directors); Industrial Research Institute (Board of Directors); Conference Board (Technology Conferences Advisory Board); National Research Council (Member, Board on Chemical Sciences and Technology); National Science Foundation (Member of the Math and Physical Sciences Advisory Boards).
- University of Maryland College of Life Sciences (Board of Visitors); University of Southern Mississippi (Distinguished Fellow of Business and Entrepreneurial Education); Institute for Strategic Business Markets, Smeal College of Business, Penn State University (Advisory Board); co-leader on two National Science Foundation grants.
- Giordan is author of more than 250 Web-based articles, print articles and presentations. She has been written about in publications including *Working Woman, Chemical Week* and *Chemical and Engineering News* and selected for inclusion in numerous Who's Who editions both nationally and internationally.

Catherine A. Gretta, Corporate Vice President Women's Markets, New York Life Insurance Company

Pearl of Wisdom: "Never say never ... I said I'd never get married, never be a life insurance agent and never travel 2 plus hours one way for a job! I have done all of these things, and they have all led to the most meaningful experiences in my life both personally and professionally."

STATS

Personal: Married, two children

Education: On-the-job training and ongoing involvement in career-related and employer-sponsored instruction and professional development courses. Life and Health Insurance Licenses — Series 63, LUTCF Designation.

Business Background & Areas of Involvement

- Previously opened, operated and sold her own bridal boutique; also a field agent for 12 years at New York Life Insurance Company prior to current position.
- Member, Million Dollar Round Table (MDRT). This is for agents in the top 10% of the industry. MDRT, an international organization recognized by the insurance industry the world over, is dedicated to the highest level of professionalism.
- 2003, nominee for Young Women's Christian Association Achievement Award; 1998/1999, Pennsylvania's "Who's Who — Women in Business;" numerous company sales awards.
- Spearheaded the development of the Women's Leadership Project and oversees the College Agent Intern and NYLIC Family programs at New York Life Insurance.
- Involved (through New York Life Insurance Company) in Women For Hire; Cornell Institute for Women and Work; and Center for Women's Business Research.
- Member, GAMA International, Life Insurance Marketing and Research Association, National Association of Life Underwriters; member, Women in Financial Services, National Association of Female Executives and National Association of Women Business Owners.

Beverly Holmes, Senior Vice President, Executive Officer, Retirement Services, MassMutual Financial Group

Pearl of Wisdom: "I have three thoughts: 'Life is passive until you make it act on your behalf'; 'Ask what you want, believe you will receive'; and "Never, ever give up on yourself or your dreams'."

STATS

Personal: One child

Education: B.A., Human Services, New Hampshire College; Master's, Education, Cambridge College; completed Excellence in Leadership Program at University of Virginia, Darden School of Business

Business Background & Areas of Involvement

- Entered the financial services business as an agent with Investors Diversified Services. She moved to administering qualified plans and developing product at Aetna Life and Casualty.
- In 2000, honored with the President's Leadership Award and promoted to Senior Vice President, Executive Officer by the MassMutual Board of Directors; in 1992, selected by *Dollars and Sense* magazine as one of "America's Best & Brightest Professional Women."
- The Collaborative Group, Inc., a nonprofit economic development organization (founder and president); Bay Path College (trustee).
- In 1995, she presented at a workshop in Hairou, China, as part of her role at the United Nations 4th World Conference on Women; in 1996, she was asked to participate in a Women's Conference Circle at the White House — sponsored by former First Lady Hillary Rodham Clinton — to discuss economic development strategies for women.
- Has published numerous articles on economic development and its impact on women in developing countries, and has traveled extensively speaking on economic and retirement issues in countries such as the People's Republic of China, Russia, Ukraine, Senegal, West Africa and England.

Irene Horstmann Hannan, Senior Vice President & Director, Women's Business Services, Wachovia

 Pearl of Wisdom: "Early on in my career, I didn't like change — it was uncomfortable. Now I understand that influencing change is what's important. Take control of the change and use your skills to direct the outcome — that's how I make a difference."

STATS

Personal: Divorced, four children

Education: BA, Trinity College; graduate coursework at Temple University and the University of Wisconsin

Business Background & Areas of Involvement

- Previously Chief Financial Officer of the National Center for Urban Ethnic Affairs in Washington, D.C.; and Vice President of Hannan Associates with offices in Washington and Philadelphia.
- 2003, appointed by Governor Rendell to the PA Commission for Women; 2003, winner of the Forum of Executive Women's Star Award"; 2002 Small Business Administration's Women's Business Advocate of the Year award; 2002, first recipient of the Iris Newman Award given by Ben Franklin Technology Center for commitment to women's entrepreneurship; 2002, named one of Pennsylvania's "Best 50 Women in Business"; 2000, "Woman of Distinction Award," from the Philadelphia Business Journal.
- Wachovia Corporate Women's Advisory Council (founding member); Temple's Fox School of Business's Center for Entrepreneurship (advisory board; named Fox School's "Executive in Residence" for 2002-2003); Women's Investment Network (board); Forum of Executive Women (Vice President)
- Crossroads School (Chairman of Board and Trustee Emeritus), Vanguard School (Trustee), Country Day School of the Sacred Heart (Trustee); St. Francis Nursing Home (lifetime board member), who granted her the Mundy Award for outstanding service; Philadelphia Chapter of Trinity College Alumnae Association (Past President); Southeastern PA Girl Scouts of America (board member).

Heidi Hunter, Vice President and Global Business Manager, Oncology, Wyeth

Pearl of Wisdom: "Don't ever think you have done enough. Help others. Be adventurous. Keep stretching."

STATS

Personal: Married, two children

Education: MBA, University of Chicago; BA Magna Cum Laude, Economics/German Language, University of Michigan

Business Background & Areas of Involvement

- Previously Vice President, Global Women's Health Care, New Products Marketing and Licensing Evaluation; prior assignments with Novo Nordisk A/S in Copenhagen, Denmark and Ciba-Geigy in Switzerland and South Africa.
- Healthcare Businesswomen's Association (member, Advisory Board).
- The Leukemia and Lymphoma Society, Eastern Pennsylvania Chapter (board); member, the American Society for Reproductive Medicine.

Christine L. James-Brown, President & CEO, United Way of Southeastern Pennsylvania

Pearl of Wisdom: "A big vision, grounded by a core set of values is of critical importance as we move through our lives. You want to stand for something … and that something you stand for (core values) should not really change over time. Push yourself and others to the outer limits of performance but never stray from the set of values that provide clarity of purpose."

STATS

Personal: Separated, one child

Education: BA, Cultural Anthropology, Douglass College; graduate work at Brown University; honorary degree, Doctor of Humane Letters, Drexel University

Business Background & Areas of Involvement

- 2002, moderator of a White House Presidential Panel on Volunteerism (President George W. Bush was a panel member); 2001, U.S. Olympic Committee torch bearer; 1998-2002, *Philadelphia Tribune* "Most Influential African Americans."
- Forum for Executive Women (member, past board member); United Way of America (member, past chair, National Professional Council)
- Board membership in the following: Community College of Philadelphia, Samuel S. Fels Foundation; Pennsylvania Bar Association Judicial Evaluation Commission; Citizens Bank; Greater Philadelphia Chamber of Commerce; Public/Private Ventures; Philadelphia School Board (served four years); United Way of America Brand Identity Committee; United Way of America Field Operations Committee; University of Pennsylvania Trustees' Council of Penn Women Celebrating a Decade of Women's Leadership, Lighting the Way: Personal Reflections of Trailblazing Women (1998 panelist)
- 2000, *Philadelphia Inquirer Magazine* cover story; 1999-2002, *Philadelphia Magazine* "Power 100 in Philadelphia"; 2000, Distinguished Daughter of Pennsylvania; 1999, National Council of Negro Women, Mary McLeod Bethune Award; 1999, B'nai B'rith Humanitarian Award.

Ellen Levine, Editor, *Good Housekeeping*

Pearl of Wisdom: "Oprah Winfrey shared with me the following quote from Maya Angelou: 'When people show you who they are the first time, believe them.'"

STATS

Personal: Married, two children

Education: BA, Political Science, Wellesley College

Business Background & Areas of Involvement

- First woman named editor-in-chief of *Good Housekeeping*.
- Previously editor-in-chief of two other major women's magazines — *Redbook* and *Woman's Day* — and was a senior editor of *Cosmopolitan*. While at *Woman's Day*, Levine also was senior vice president of Hachette Magazines, Inc.
- In 1986, the American Society of Journalists and Authors presented her with an award for courage in the pursuit of truth; in 1987, similarly honored by the Atlantic Coast Independent Distributors, Inc. for distinguished service in defending the First Amendment of the U.S. Constitution; in 1999, *Good Housekeeping* won the National Magazine Award in the category of Personal Service; recognized by the American Health Foundation in 1996, and served as a delegate at the International Women's Media Foundation meeting in the Czech Republic.
- American Society of Magazine Editors (two terms as president); member of the U.S. Attorney General's Commission on Pornography.
- New York Restoration Project (board member); Lifetime Television (board member); Research America (board member); New York Women in Communications (board of advisors); consulting editor of *O, The Oprah Magazine*.
- Frequent guest on national talk shows and news programs; author of books and articles. Her work has appeared in many publications, including *The New York Times*.

Aida Levitan, Ph.D., Co-Chairperson & CEO, Publicis Sanchez & Levitan

Pearl of Wisdom: "If you want to be successful and influential, you must be passionately committed to the path you have chosen and tenacious enough so that obstacles do not discourage you. Passion, commitment to a vision and staying on course are major qualities of the true leader."

STATS

Personal: Divorced, one child

Education: Ph.D., Spanish Literature, Emory University; B.A., Magna Cum Laude, University of Miami

Business Background & Areas of Involvement

- Formerly City of Miami Director of Information and Visitors, and a Spanish literature college professor.
- Developed an award-winning, national concert series with Oscar-nominated actor Andy Garcia, to celebrate the contributions of Cachao, the creator of the Cuban jam session. The *Cachao Mambo and Descarga* Cuban Music Series produced by her agency, under her direction, won the national PRSA Multicultural Excellence Award and resulted in a film.
- 2000, Publicis Sanchez & Levitan was named one of the Top Employers of Working Women in Florida by the State of Florida Commission on the Status of Women; 1999 winner, Hispanic magazine *Adelante* National Award; 1996 winner, Top Women Achievers of South Florida.
- Association of Hispanic Advertising Agencies (board member; President, 2003-2004); member, Public Relations Society of America (PRSA) and its Counselors Academy; Miami Art Museum (Board of Trustees); Cuban-American National Council (board); Public Policy/Advocacy Committee of the Association of Hispanic Advertising Agencies (chairperson); member, American Advertising Federation Business Practices Committee; created the Coalition of Hispanic-American Women.

Ada C. Nielsen, Manager, Commercial Development, Nitriles Licensing, BP Chemicals

 Pearl of Wisdom: "Do the right thing. It doesn't always work out to your immediate career advantage, but it leads to a more developed human being, ready for the long stretch of living your life. Try to be more interested in giving back rather than taking."

STATS

Personal: Married, two children

Education: AB, Chemistry, Wellesley; MBA, finance and marketing, University of Chicago Graduate School of Business; studied theoretical physical chemistry in graduate programs at Tulane University and Dartmouth College.

Business Background & Areas of Involvement

- Previously, she founded Capstone International to specialize in opportunity analysis, business development, strategic marketing, technology transfer, market and competitive analysis, and worked in marketing, sales, and finance positions for Fortune 500 companies.
- Commercial Development and Management Association (CDMA, Educational Foundation Chair 2002-2003); Chicago CDMA Chapter (current chair, president-elect, 2003); member, American Chemical Society; Association for Corporate Growth; Association for Strategic Alliance Professionals; Association for University Technology Managers; European Chemicals Marketing & Strategy Association; Federation of Societies for Coatings Technology; Strategic Management Association; and Women Advancing Bio.
- Licensing Executives Society International (LESI) (Vice-Chairman of Education, 2001-2002); LES/USA-Canada (trustee); member of the Education Committee, steering committee member, Energy, Chemicals, & Polymers Committee; and a member of the Intellectual Property Owners Association Taxation and Valuation Committee.
- In 2002, named to the Illinois Board of Natural Resources & Conservation (confirmed by the Illinois Senate), where she serves on the Human Resources Committee and chairs an ad hoc committee on intellectual property.

Dr. Catherine E. Palmier, Chief Medical Officer, United Healthcare of Georgia

Pearl of Wisdom: "Never underestimate the value of wisdom and advice from others. Seek mentors and champions for your cause. I am fortunate to be married to my best mentor!!"

STATS

Personal: Married, three children (including twins!)

Education: BA, Cell Biology, SUNY at Buffalo; MD, Upstate Medical Center, Syracuse, New York; Residency in Pediatrics, St. Christopher's Hospital for Children; MA, Organizational Management, University of Phoenix; Board Certified in Pediatrics

Business Background & Areas of Involvement

- Previously Regional Medical Director in Philadelphia, Dallas, and Atlanta for Aetna, Inc.; Director of Community Inpatient Pediatrics at The Children's Hospital of Philadelphia; and a primary care pediatrician in a group practice with The University of Maryland.
- Received the "Governor's Award for Volunteerism" from Texas Governor Ann Richards in 1993.
- Co-founder and Volunteer Medical Director of the Southeast Texas Community Health Clinic; American Academy of Pediatrics (fellow); member, The American College of Physician Executives.

Peggie Pelosi-Gardiner, Vice President of Network Development, USANA Health Sciences

 Pearl of Wisdom: "Here are some of my favorite expressions: 'Life is a work in progress … live it by design, not by default'; 'On the river of life, take out your oars and paddle. Otherwise you'll get swept along by the current and end up somewhere you just may not want to be'; and 'Purpose is stronger than outcome … Reasons come first, answers come second.'"

STATS

Personal: Married, five children

Education: Degree, Media Arts Business Administration, Trebas Institute for the Recording Arts in Toronto, Canada

Business Background & Areas of Involvement

- Previously, General Manager for Discovery Toys Canada; and the first International Blue Diamond Executive with NuSkin International, Inc.
- Children's Hanger Fund (member, board of directors); Unstoppable Foundation (fundraiser).
- As a speaker, has educated, motivated and celebrated tens of thousands of independent network marketing distributors around the world.
- Co-founder of Providence Music Group, "created to discover, develop and promote music for a better world."

Janice Price, President and CEO, The Kimmel Center for the Performing Arts

Pearl of Wisdom: "As you're building your career, don't ever get so attached to your 'plan' that you miss the opportunities that may be making themselves available on the sidelines. You may be offered a chance to learn something new or take on a task that doesn't precisely match where you saw yourself being at that moment in your career trajectory."

STATS

Personal: Canadian, divorced, no children

Education: BA, History and Politics, Trinity College of the University of Toronto

Business Background & Areas of Involvement

- Formerly interim executive director and Vice President of Marketing and Communications at New York's Lincoln Center for the Performing Arts.
- Chamber of Commerce (board); PCVB Executive Committee (board); Pennsylvania Travel and Tourism Partnership (Governor's Appointee); Performing Arts Center Consortium; The League of American Theatres and Producers; International Society for the Performing Arts; International Presenters Network; International Association of Assembly Managers.

Elizabeth "Lisa" Reeves, Senior Vice President, SAP Ventures

Pearl of Wisdom: "Early in your career, take risks. Take on difficult projects; those that are complex, political or time consuming. If you succeed, you will garner significant visibility and reward in your organization while also building tremendous self-confidence."

STATS

Personal: Married, two children

Education: MBA, American Graduate School of International Management ("Thunderbird"); BA, Economics, Kalamazoo College

Business Background & Areas of Involvement
- Previously served in numerous senior executive positions in business development, product marketing, sales and consulting, in SAP America; before joining SAP, held various operational roles in strategic planning, finance and market research at the Chrysler Corporation.
- APICS certification.
- Active in several Rocky Mountain-based organizations, charities and companies.

Jo Anne Rolle Harper, Vice President, Steere Pharmaceuticals, Pfizer Inc.

Pearl of Wisdom: "Work hard. Work smart. Become the go-to expert in your market and on your team. Be accountable, set your bar high and have fun."

STATS

Personal: Married, two stepchildren

Education: BS, Merchandising, double minor in Marketing and Chemistry, University of Arizona

Business Background & Areas of Involvement

- Previously worked at Ryan Insurance Group in Chicago; and at I. Magnin and Company in San Francisco.
- Three-time Vice President's Management Council Award Winner.
- Juvenile Diabetes Research Foundation, Fairfield, CT; Luminaires Support Group, Orange County, CA.

Michelle "Shelley" Rosen, Senior Director Strategy, Business Development, McDonald's Corporation

 Pearl of Wisdom: "Take control of your life and realize this is not a dress rehearsal. We have one chance to live the life we dream by realizing we control our own destiny in work, at home and play. Surround yourself with people you enjoy and things you like doing. and success and joy in achievement will follow."

STATS
Personal: Single

Education: BA, University of Michigan

Business Background & Areas of Involvement
- Most of Rosen's 20-year career has been spent working for leading global advertising agencies developing new relationships and managing global multi-national brands. One of those clients was McDonald's Corporation.
- Founder of "Pink Think," a women's network designed to build confidence in women to network to achieve their dreams; Promotion Marketing Association (board); Columbia College (board).

Catherine J. Ross, President, Security Services, Day & Zimmermann

Pearl of Wisdom: "There are many obstacles along a career path, but perseverance, hard work and a sense of humor, will help remove those obstacles."

STATS

Personal: Married

Education: BA, Criminal Justice, University of South Florida

Business Background & Areas of Involvement

- Previously Vice President of Operations/National Accounts for The Wackenhut Corp.
- Certified in TQM, Total Quality Management.
- Fundraiser for Muscular Dystrophy Association, Multiple Sclerosis Society and several local charities.
- Member, International Security Management Association and American Society for Industrial Security.
- Writes articles for company newsletter; gives company-related presentations.

Diana K. Ruddick, Vice President, Distribution Development & Communications, MassMutual Financial Group

Pearl of Wisdom: "If you're unselfish in helping other people get what they want, they'll be there to help you get what you want later on."

STATS

Personal: Divorced, one child

Education: BA, French, Summa Cum Laude, Indiana University

Business Background & Areas of Involvement

- Previously, Director of Managed Healthcare at Aetna Life & Casualty.
- Honored with MassMutual Financial Group's "President's Leadership Award."
- Member, MassMutual Financial Group's Leadership Effectiveness Board; Diversity Committee; Brand Advisory Board; and Women's Business Advisory Board.

Sue Rusch, President, Direct Sales Resources, Inc.

Pearl of Wisdom: "Trust your instincts! Much business success stems from reading circumstances and drawing upon our 'gut level' feelings about the right course of action to take."

STATS

Personal: Married, three children

Education: Two years of college; participates in professional development opportunities within her industry.

Business Background & Areas of Involvement

- Previously, was Senior Executive Sales Director with The Pampered Chef.
- Earned many honors at The Pampered Chef, including prestigious Legacy Award (charter recipient), Circle of Honor, and served two terms on the Long-Term Planning Committee.
- National Speakers Association, Minnesota Chapter (Vice President).
- Candidate for CSP (Certified Speaking Professional) designation from the National Speakers Association.
- Successful speaker and executive coach.

Molly D. Shepard, President & CEO, The Leader's Edge

Pearl of Wisdom: "A truly effective leader is one who is genuinely interested and involved in helping with the issues, problems and lives of her stakeholders, customers and friends."

STATS

Personal: Married, three children

Education: BS, Wheaton College; MS, Psychological Services and Counseling, University of Pennsylvania

Business Background & Areas of Involvement

- Previously, Chairman, President and Co-founder of Manchester, Inc., one of the world's largest career development consulting firms. Prior to co-founding Manchester, Inc., she was regional Vice President for Hay Career Consultants, a division of the Hay Group, an international management consulting firm.
- Founded *The Leader's Edge*™, a Philadelphia-based company that promotes the advancement of high level executive women through leadership development.
- 2003, Montgomery County March of Dimes "Woman of Achievement"; 2002 winner, Elizabeth Campbell Award as "Outstanding Public Broadcasting Volunteer of the Year"; 2001 winner, Paradigm Award, presented by the Greater Philadelphia Chamber of Commerce to a businesswoman whose outstanding professional and personal achievements serve as a model for success; 2001 "Best 50 Women in Business in Pennsylvania"; 1998, the American Heart Association's "Heart of Philadelphia Award" for leadership and dedication to the community.
- WHYY-TV 12 (PBS) (Chairman); United Way of Southeastern Pennsylvania (Chairman 2001-2003); World Affairs Council (Secretary); Pennsylvania Women's Forum (President 2000-2002); National Multiple Sclerosis Society (board); Greater Philadelphia Chamber of Commerce (Vice Chairman; board and Executive Committee).
- Shepard has published numerous articles and is a frequent speaker at various meetings and conferences throughout the country.

Betty L. Siegel, Ph.D., President, Kennesaw State University

Pearl of Wisdom: "How do we define a phenomenal woman? We might begin by saying that she is strong in her beliefs and her person, that she is a community role model, that she is a servant in the most ennobling sense of the word. That she serves her cause well, with the goal of lifting others up and making the world a better place. In defining her, we might echo Sojourner Truth: 'Ain't she a woman?'"

STATS

Personal: Married, two children, two grandchildren

Education: Ph.D., Florida State University; M.Ed., University of North Carolina at Chapel Hill; BA, Wake Forest University; Associate of Arts, Cumberland College. Two years, post-doctoral study, Indiana University. Honorary doctorates from Cumberland College in Kentucky, Miami University in Ohio, Eastern Kentucky University and Lynchburg College and Morehead State University.

Business Background & Areas of Involvement

- First woman to head an institution in the 34-unit University System of Georgia.
- 2003, received the Peabody Award, the highest distinguished alumni award presented by the School of Education of the University of North Carolina at Chapel Hill; listed repeatedly by *Georgia Trend* among the 100 most influential Georgians; Influential Atlantans by the *Atlanta Business Chronicle*; 1996, Cobb; "1997 Georgia Woman of the Year;" 1969, Distinguished Teacher of the Year Award at the University of Florida.
- International Alliance for Invitational Education (co-founder and co-director); American Association of State Colleges and Universities (former chair); American Council on Education (former director); Business-Higher Education Forum (member, Executive Committee); American Humanics, Inc. (secretary and board); American Institute for Managing Diversity (board).
- Member of board for: Atlanta Ballet; Boy Scouts of Atlanta; CDC Foundation; SafeAmerica, Inc. (founding chair); The Southern Institute for Business and Professional Ethics; WellStar Kennestone Hospital Foundation; and the Cobb Chamber of Commerce.
- Delivers keynote addresses and provides consulting to hundreds of international, national, regional and state affiliations.

Catherine "Cathy" Angell Sohn, Pharm.D., Vice President Worldwide Business Development, Consumer Healthcare, GlaxoSmithKline

Pearl of Wisdom: "Build or get on a strong team. With a strong team, behind a common vision, anything is possible. Praise your team members and leader often to others. It will enhance the image and success of the entire team and reflect well on you."

STATS

Personal: Married, two children

Education: Doctor of Pharmacy from University of California, San Francisco, School of Pharmacy

Business Background & Areas of Involvement

- Previously, served on faculty at the Philadelphia College of Pharmacy; completed a residency at UCSF; and also edited the Drug Bulletin at Kaiser Permanente in San Francisco.
- Named "2003 Woman of the Year" by the Healthcare Businesswomen's Association.
- Serves on the Health Advisory Board for Johns Hopkins Bloomberg School of Public Health, and on the Board of Directors for World Self Medication Industry.
- Published more than six book chapters and 15 articles on infectious disease, clinical pharmacy, OBGyn, and nonprescription drug topics; former editor of Kaiser Permanente's *Drug Bulletin*.

Lynn A. Tetrault, Esq., Vice President of Human Resources, AstraZeneca

Pearl of Wisdom: "When you communicate, remember that you are the message. Be yourself and lead with courage."

STATS

Personal: Married, two children

Education: BS, magna cum laude, Princeton University; law degree, University of Virginia Law School

Business Background & Areas of Involvement

- Previously Tetrault practiced law with the Boston firm Choate, Hall and Stewart, where she specialized in corporate and healthcare law.
- 2002, Human Resources department at AstraZeneca recognized as HR Department of the Year in the Tri-State Area by The Rosen Group; 2001, awarded Delaware Valley HR Person of the Year from Society for Human Resource Management (SHRM).
- Human Resource Planning Society (board); SHRM (member, Senior Communication Council).
- Ronald McDonald House of Delaware (President's Advisory Council).

Judith E. Tschirgi, Chief Information Officer & Senior Vice President, SEI Investments

 Pearl of Wisdom: "Career success ultimately depends on your ability to deliver business value, but timing, visibility and sponsorship are critical. You must make yourself 'top-of-mind' to those executives who can help you when opportunities for advancement arise."

STATS

Personal: Married, two children

Education: B.A., Experimental Psychology, Stanford University; Ph.D., Experimental Psychology, University of California, San Diego

Business Background & Areas of Involvement

- Previously at AT&T Bell Laboratories (now Lucent Technology) for 16 years. While at AT&T, she was Director of the Advanced Speech Technology Department.
- Received numerous AT&T awards, including Arno Penzias award for successful technology transfer.
- 2001, named one of 50 Women of the Millennium by Feminine Fortunes in partnership with The Vital Voices Democracy Initiative.
- Member of the Board of the Pennsylvania Economy League; sponsor of Lenfest High School (Philadelphia High Tech High School program); participates in Philadelphia Chapter of The Content of our Character, an ethics mentoring program for young professionals.

Susan F. Ward, Vice President, United Parcel Service, Inc. (UPS)

Pearl of Wisdom: "Shoot for the Moon. Even if you miss, you will land among the stars."

STATS

Personal: Married, two children

Education: BBA, Magna Cum Laude, Accounting, St. Bonaventure University; MBA, Finance, Fordham University; holds a Certified Professional Accountant licensure

Business Background & Areas of Involvement

- Previously worked in the Audit practice of Ernst & Young.
- Serves on the boards of three UPS captive insurance companies; member of the UPS Corporate Compliance Committee and has served on the UPS Diversity Committee.
- Georgia Society of CPAs (member); AIG International Advisory Board (member).
- Queen of Angels Catholic School (Vice Chairperson, Chairperson Development Committee); very active in her church, serving in several ministries.
- Guest speaker at 2002 International Aviation Women's Association meeting, where she spoke on "Insurance in the Aviation World"; in March 2002, spoke on the topic "Corporate Crisis Management in the Wake of September 11, 2001," at the annual UPS Management Conference for the company's senior level executives.